KT-406-404

NATIONS OF THE WORLD

INDIA

Anita Dalal

www.raintreepublishers.co.uk
Visit our website to find out more information about Raintree books.

To order:
 Phone 44 (0) 1865 888113
 Send a fax to 44 (0) 1865 314091
Visit the Raintree bookshop at www.raintreepublishers.co.uk to browse our catalogue and order online.

Produced for Raintree by the Brown Reference Group plc
Project Editor: Peter Jones
Designer: Joan Curtis
Cartographer: William Le Bihan
Picture Researcher: Liz Clachan
Editorial Assistant: Anthony Shaw
Indexer: Kay Ollerenshaw

Raintree Publishers
Editors: Isabel Thomas and Kate Buckingham

Printed and bound in Singapore.

ISBN 1 844 21469 9
07 06 05 04 03
10 9 8 7 6 5 4 3 2 1

British Library cataloguing in publication data
Dalal, Anita
    India – (Nations of the world)
    1. Human geography – India –
    Juvenile literature
    2. India – Geography – Juvenile
    literature
    I. Title
    915.4

A full catalogue is available for this book from the British Library.

Acknowledgements
Front cover: Palace of Jaipur
Title page: The Red Fort, Delhi

The acknowledgements on page 128 form part of this copyright page.

Every effort has been made to contact copyright holders of any material reproduced in this book. Any omissions will be rectified in subsequent printings if notice is given to the publishers.

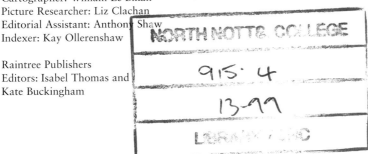

Contents

Foreword

S ince ancient times, people have gathered together in communities where they could share and trade resources and strive to build a safe and happy environment. Gradually, as populations grew and societies became more complex, communities expanded to become nations – groups of people who felt sufficiently bound by a common heritage to work together for a shared future.

Land has usually played an important role in defining a nation. People have a natural affection for the landscape in which they grew up. They are proud of its natural beauties – the mountains, rivers and forests – and of the towns and cities that flourish there. People are proud, too, of their nation's history – the shared struggles and achievements that have shaped the way they live today.

Religion, culture, race and lifestyle, too, have sometimes played a role in fostering a nation's identity. Often, though, a nation includes people of different races, beliefs and customs. Many may have come from distant countries. Nations have rarely been fixed, unchanging things, either territorially or racially. Throughout history, borders have changed, often under the pressure of war, and people have migrated across the globe in search of a new life or because they are fleeing from oppression or disaster. The world's nations are still changing today: some nations are breaking up and new nations are forming.

Indian civilization is one of the oldest in the world, and first formed around the banks of the Indus River over 4000 years ago. It was in India that two of the world's major religions, Hinduism and Buddhism, emerged. Although protected by the towering Himalayan Mountains to the north, the subcontinent's fertile river plains and thriving agriculture attracted invaders. India's southern coasts played a major part in medieval trade with China and Europe, and from the 18th century until independence in 1947, it was ruled by the British. Recently the country has worked hard to overcome problems of poverty and underdevelopment, while maintaining the incredible richness of its cultural traditions.

Introduction

 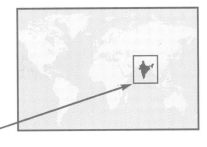

India is one of the world's most colourful, exciting and varied places. The country's history stretches back thousands of years. It has an economy based on the latest modern technology as well as centuries-old farming methods; and India is home to a multitude of different religions and languages. In 1897, the American writer Mark Twain (1835–1910) described India as: 'the land of dreams and romance, of fabulous wealth and fabulous poverty, of splendour and rags, of palaces and hovels, of famine and pestilence, of genies and giants and Aladdin lamps, of tigers and elephants, the cobra and the jungle, the country of a hundred nations and a hundred tongues, of a thousand religions and two million gods ...'. Twain's description is still accurate today.

Walk down any busy street in the country's capital, Delhi, and you might see a business executive talking on her mobile phone, while a holy man, dressed in yellow robes, sits on the pavement receiving alms. Poor dwellings exist next door to luxury high-rise apartments. It is possible to travel from the wettest city in the world to some of the world's driest deserts – and still be in India.

India lies in southern Asia and most of the country is surrounded by ocean: the Arabian Sea to the west, the Bay of Bengal to the east and the Indian Ocean to the south. The country's northern border is formed by the highest mountain range in the world, the Himalayas.

Jodhpur in Rajasthan in north-east India is often called the Blue City.
Blue was traditionally the colour of the houses of Brahmins, or holy men.

FACT FILE

- India is the world's most populous democracy.

- India has the second-largest population in the world and is projected to overtake China by 2030.

- India is home to two of the world's major religions – **Hinduism** and Buddhism.

- Indians call their country *Bharat Mata* ('Mother India').

- **Hindi** is the third-most spoken language in the world after Mandarin Chinese and English.

- The cost of living in India is 30% of that in the United Kingdom.

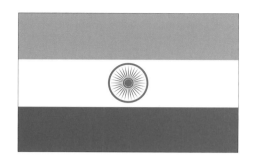

Known as the 'tricolour', India's flag is made up of three equal horizontal bands of colour. The top band is saffron, representing Hinduism, the green band represents Islam and the central white band represents all other religions.

The rupee comes in 500, 100, 50, 20, 10, 5, 2 and 1 notes, but the 5, 2 and 1 notes are being phased out.

MOTHER INDIA

Modern-day India's size and boundaries date from 1947, when the country gained independence from Great Britain. The country's administrative regions are the result of historical divisions between different religions, and of the different princely states that existed before independence (see page 59). The centuries' old conflict between the members of two religions, Hinduism and **Islam**, has dominated much of India's history. At the beginning of the 21st century, India and its **Muslim** neighbour, Pakistan, continue to argue over the future of the northern state of Kashmir (see page 16), which both countries claim as their own.

India is a federal **republic** made up of 28 states and seven union territories. It is a democracy – that is, its government is elected by the people. In practice, however, one political party, the Congress Party, was the major party in government from 1947 until the elections of 1996, when the Hindu nationalist party, the BJP, became the largest party represented in the government.

India's tricolour flag has a 24-spoke wheel (*chakra*) in the centre white band. The *chakra* is a symbol from the reign of India's first great emperor, Asoka, who became ruler of India in 272 BC (see page 48). The design of the wheel is based on the Asokan pillar at Sarnath, the city where the founder of the Buddhist religion, the Buddha (see page 114), first preached. After India became independent from Britain in 1947, the tricolour flag was created to symbolize an independent India.

The currency of India is the rupee. On the back of the rupee notes, the value is written in India's official languages (see opposite) – Marathi and the ancient written language of **Sanskrit** are missing from the list.

The national anthem

The words of India's national anthem were written by the Nobel Prize-winning author Rabindranath Tagore and were first sung on 27 December 1911. The song was adopted as the national anthem for the newly independent India on 24 January 1950. Only the first verse of the five-verse song is used in the current national anthem. Tagore translated the song into English himself. Before then, the Indian anthem had been 'I Bow to the Motherland' ('Vanda Mataram'), which was sung at Indian Congress Party meetings during India's fight for independence from Britain (see pages 66–67). But India's first prime minister after independence, Jawaharlal Nehru, felt the old anthem was inappropriate.

'Jana Gana Mana'
Thou art the ruler of the minds of all
    people, dispenser of India's destiny.
Thy name rouses the hearts of Punjab,
    Sind, Gujarat and Maratha,
Of the Dravida and Orissa and Bengal;
It echoes in the hills of Vindhyas and
    Himalaya,
Mingles in the music of Yamuna and
    Ganges,
And is chanted by the waves of the
    Indian Sea.
They pray for thy blessings and sing thy
    praise.
The saving of all people waits in thy
    hand,
Thou dispenser of India's destiny,
Victory, victory, victory to thee.

LANGUAGES AND PEOPLE

The national language of India is Hindi, which is the first language of 30 per cent of the population, most of whom live in the north. There are sixteen other official languages, each with its own script, and most of these are spoken in specific regions. For example, in the eastern state of Bengal, Bengali is the main language. Apart from Hindi, India's other official languages are: Assamese, Bengali, Gujarati, Kannada, Kashmiri, Konkani, Malayalam, Marathi, Nepali, Oriya, Punjabi, Sanskrit, Sindhi, Tamil, Telugu and Urdu.

In addition to the official languages, there are more than 1000 other languages and dialects. (A dialect is a variation of a language.) India is one of the few countries in the world where two of its citizens might not be able to understand each other's language.

Modern English has borrowed many words from the languages of the Indian subcontinent, including dungarees, khaki, pyjamas, sandals, shampoo and verandah.

India is still largely a rural country. Although poverty exists in both urban and rural communities, the villages in rural India provide a better system of support than the crowded shanties of India's cities.

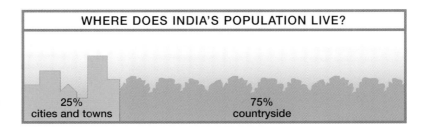

WHERE DOES INDIA'S POPULATION LIVE?

25% cities and towns

75% countryside

English was brought to India by the British rulers, and for many years it was the language that all educated Indians spoke. Today, English continues to be the most important language for business and international communication and is the official language of the legal profession. The Indian government's attempts to replace English with Hindi in schools, universities and offices have failed because the languages of south India bear little relation to Hindi, and southern Indians prefer to speak English rather than Hindi. Throughout India, middle-class parents prefer their children to learn English, as well as their regional language, because they believe learning English will help the children in their future careers. Indian English is often nicknamed 'Hinglish' because it is English with a peculiarly Indian choice of words. To catch a criminal in Hinglish, for instance, is to 'nab a miscreant'.

The Indian population originates from two main ethnic groups: Indo-Aryan and Dravidian. The Dravidians are the original inhabitants of India, while the Indo-Aryans invaded India around 1500 BC, pushing the Dravidians south (see page 45).

India has the second-largest population in the world after China. Its population rose rapidly in the second half of the 20th century. In 1947, at the time of Indian independence, the population was over 300 million.

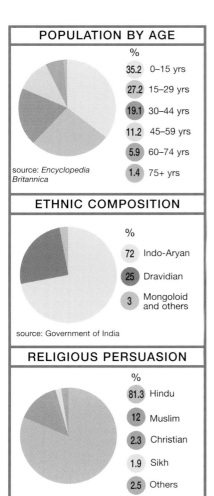

POPULATION BY AGE

%

35.2 0–15 yrs

27.2 15–29 yrs

19.1 30–44 yrs

11.2 45–59 yrs

5.9 60–74 yrs

1.4 75+ yrs

source: *Encyclopedia Britannica*

ETHNIC COMPOSITION

%

72 Indo-Aryan

25 Dravidian

3 Mongoloid and others

source: Government of India

RELIGIOUS PERSUASION

%

81.3 Hindu

12 Muslim

2.3 Christian

1.9 Sikh

2.5 Others

source: Government of India

POPULATION DENSITY

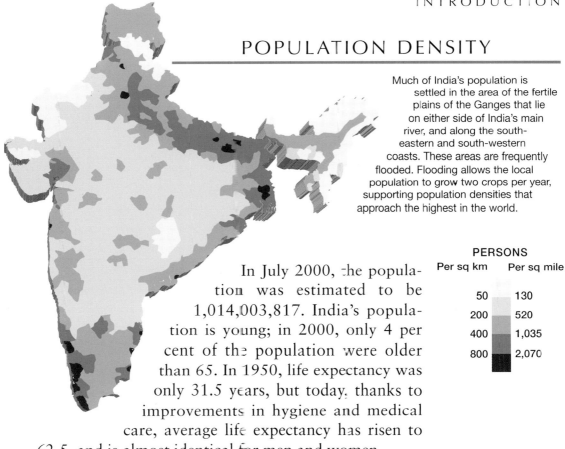

Much of India's population is settled in the area of the fertile plains of the Ganges that lie on either side of India's main river, and along the south-eastern and south-western coasts. These areas are frequently flooded. Flooding allows the local population to grow two crops per year, supporting population densities that approach the highest in the world.

PERSONS

Per sq km	Per sq mile
50	130
200	520
400	1,035
800	2,070

In July 2000, the population was estimated to be 1,014,003,817. India's population is young; in 2000, only 4 per cent of the population were older than 65. In 1950, life expectancy was only 31.5 years, but today, thanks to improvements in hygiene and medical care, average life expectancy has risen to 62.5, and is almost identical for men and women.

Religion: a part of life

Religion is woven into every aspect of life in India, although there is no state (or official) religion. The country is the birthplace of two of the world's oldest religions – Hinduism and Buddhism. Today, 80 per cent of Indians are Hindu, 12 per cent are Muslim, 2.3 per cent Christian, about 2 per cent Sikh and 0.8 per cent are Buddhist. Jainism, one of the world's smallest religions, is almost exclusive to India (see page 115). Jainism originated in the country at around the same time as Buddhism and comprises 0.5 per cent of the population.

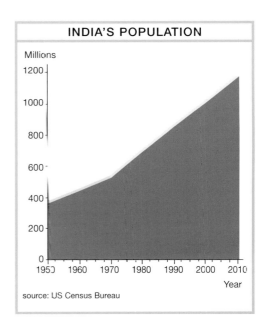

INDIA'S POPULATION

source: US Census Bureau

Land and Cities

"If there is one place on the face of the earth where all the dreams of living men have found a home from the very earliest days when man began the dream of existence, it is India."

French scholar Romain Rolland

India is more than six times the area of France. It lies within the Indian subcontinent, which is bigger than Europe. From the snow-covered peaks of the Himalayan Mountains in the north to India's tropical southern tip is a distance of some 5600 kilometres (3500 miles). The country is divided almost exactly in two by the Tropic of Cancer.

India is the largest country in the Indian subcontinent. Before India gained independence from the British in 1947 (see page 70), the country was even bigger because the present-day countries of Bangladesh and Pakistan then lay within its borders. India is the seventh-largest country in the world after Russia, Canada, China, the USA, Brazil and Australia. India's total land area is approximately 3,287,590 square kilometres (2,042,870 square miles).

India shares land borders with Bangladesh, Bhutan, Myanmar (Burma), China, Nepal and Pakistan in the north, and is bordered by sea to the west, south and east. India's mountainous north has traditionally given it a certain amount of protection against invasion, while its coastal areas have since ancient times been important in international trade. Part of the north-western region is also claimed by Pakistan. India is also in dispute with China over territory along its north-eastern border, which was taken by China in conflicts in the 1960s.

Women wash clothes on the banks of Lake Bhutanatha in Karnataka state in south-west India, as their ancestors have done for centuries.

FACT FILE

- The Himalayan Mountains, which form part of India's northern border, are the highest in the world, although the highest mountain, Everest, lies in Nepal and China.

- The Ganges Plain, in eastern India, is the largest river plain in the world.

- The Asiatic lion is found in only one place in the world – the Gir National Park in the western state of Gujarat.

- A banyan tree in the botanical gardens in Kolkata (Calcutta) has the largest canopy of any tree in the world with a circumference of over 400 m (1300 ft).

13

Mountains
The highest mountain range in the world, the Himalayas stretch into neighbouring Pakistan, Nepal, Bhutan and China. The mountains were created by the Indian peninsula moving northwards and thrusting up against the Eurasian Plate – a process that is still happening.

Deccan Plateau
This plateau forms the bulk of the peninsula between the Arabian Sea and the Bay of Bengal. It averages between 305 and 762 m (1000 and 2500 ft) above sea level.

Eastern and Western Ghats
These mountain ranges lie along India's south-eastern and south-western coasts. Those in the west are higher and include the Nilgiri Hills, where the highest peak stands at 2695 m (8842 ft).

INDIA'S TERRAIN

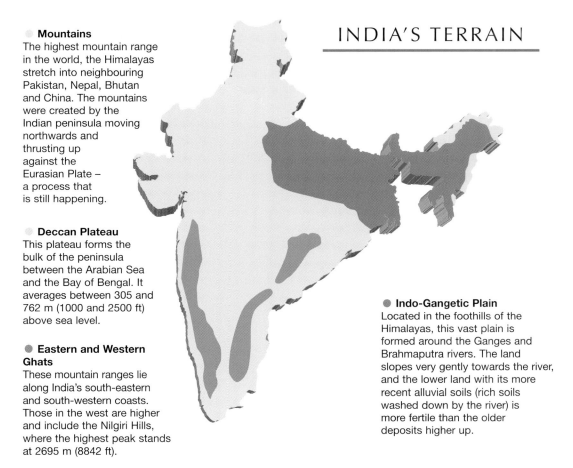

Indo-Gangetic Plain
Located in the foothills of the Himalayas, this vast plain is formed around the Ganges and Brahmaputra rivers. The land slopes very gently towards the river, and the lower land with its more recent alluvial soils (rich soils washed down by the river) is more fertile than the older deposits higher up.

A LAND OF CONTRASTS

Almost every variation in geography and climate exists within India. In the frozen Himalayan Mountains are glaciers; in the western states of Gujarat and Rajasthan is the Thar Desert, one of the driest places on Earth. To the east in Meghalaya are the world's two wettest cities, Cherrapunji and Mawsynram. The Ganges Plain, in the east, is one of the world's most fertile places. The tapering southern part of India comprises the Deccan Plateau, bordered on both sides by mountains known as the Western and Eastern Ghats.

The roof of the world

The Himalayas create a massive natural barrier between India and its huge neighbour, China. The mountain range stretches 2484 kilometres (1553 miles) from the

The Himalayas are named from the Sanskrit words *hima*, meaning 'snow', and *laya*, meaning 'abode'.

state of Jammu and Kashmir in the north-west to the state of Assam in the south-east. From north to south, the mountains are between 148 and 400 kilometres (93 and 250 miles) wide. The Himalayas actually comprise three parallel ranges of mountains. It is the youngest mountain range in the world, having started to form about 40 million years ago. More than 90 per cent of the Himalayan peaks stand over 6000 metres (19,685 feet). India's highest mountain – and the third highest in

The Himalayas are sacred to Buddhists, who build cairns (piles of stones) to mark the most sacred places.

the world – Kangchenjunga, is 8586 metres (28,169 feet) high. The highest mountains in the Himalayas are covered in snow all year. Between the mountain ranges are deep gorges and valleys that are home to many people.

Many of the most important rivers of the subcontinent originate in the snowy Himalayas. The Ganges River, considered holy by the country's Hindu population, starts in the mountains as pure, melted snow before flowing southwards through India and turning eastwards to empty into the Bay of Bengal. The Ganges is joined by many other rivers on its journey south. It is 2511 kilometres (1560 miles) long. The seasonal flow of the Ganges, with its melted water flowing down from the Himalayas, makes it an important irrigation resource for the surrounding region.

The state of Kashmir

One of the most beautiful states in all of the Himalayas is Kashmir. It is home to the Kashmir goat, which provides the wool for one of the world's most expensive materials – cashmere. When the Mughals ruled India (see page 52), they would go to the mountains to escape from the heat in Delhi, where temperatures often reached 40 °C (104 °F). Their favourite place was Kashmir. Later, the British rulers also escaped the heat of the plains and headed for higher elevations, known as hill stations, where they built summer homes. However, the ruler, or **maharaja**, of Kashmir forbade the British to build houses on his land. Instead, they built luxurious houseboats, which they moored on the large lake in Srinagar, the state capital. After the British left India, the houseboats became popular with Indian honeymooners and foreign travellers.

After independence in 1947, there was tension between India and Pakistan over which country should own Kashmir. Kashmir had Hindu rulers but a predominantly **Muslim** population. Pakistan, which is a Muslim country, thought Kashmir should be part of its territory, and India, which is mainly Hindu, claimed it as its own. The two countries went to war immediately after India's independence and on three subsequent occasions, in 1965–66, 1971 and 1999. Kashmiri separatists, who want to make Kashmir an independent nation, joined the conflict. Today, India and Pakistan are still in dispute over the region.

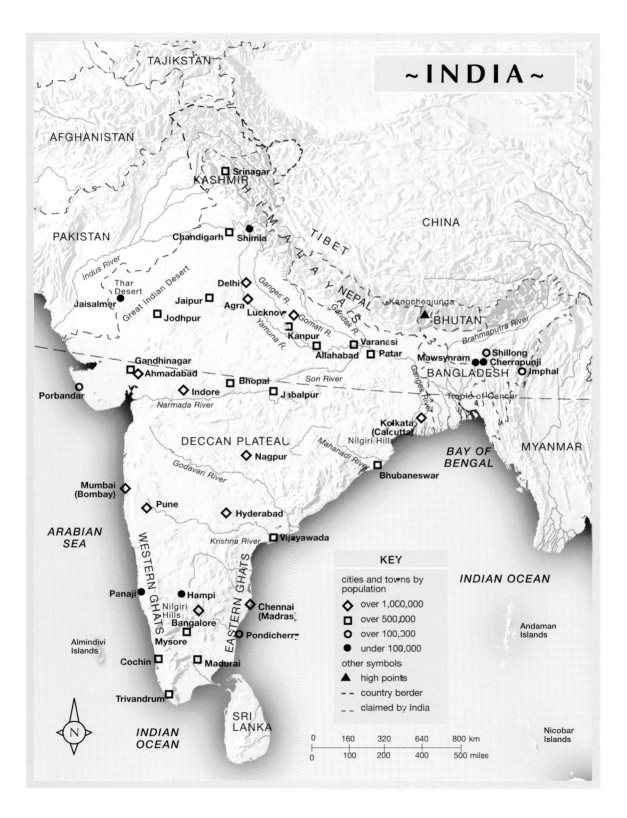

~INDIA~

TAJIKISTAN

AFGHANISTAN

PAKISTAN

CHINA

KASHMIR

■ Srinagar

Chandigarh □ ● Shimla

TIBET

Indus River

Thar
Desert
Jaisalmer ●

Great Indian Desert

NEPAL

H I M A L A Y A S

Delhi ◆
Jaipur □
Agra ◆
Jodhpur □
Lucknow ◆
Kanpur ◆
Allahabad ◆
Varanasi □
Patar □

Ganges R.
Gomati R.
Gandak R.
Yamuna R.

Kangchenjunga
▲
BHUTAN

Brahmaputra River

Mawsynram ●
Shillong ○
Cherrapunji ●
Imphal ○

BANGLADESH

Gandhinagar □
◆ Ahmadabad

Bhopal □
◆ Indore

Porbandar ○

Narmada River

Son River

Jabalpur □

Ganges River

Tropic of Cancer

DECCAN PLATEAU

◆ Nagpur

Godavari River

Mahanadi River

Kolkata
(Calcutta) ◆
Nilgiri Hills

BAY OF
BENGAL

MYANMAR

Bhubaneswar □

Mumbai ◆
(Bombay)

◆ Pune

◆ Hyderabad

ARABIAN
SEA

Krishna River

◆ Vijayawada

WESTERN GHATS

Panaji ● ● Hampi
Nilgiri
Hills

EASTERN GHATS

◆ Chennai
(Madras)

INDIAN OCEAN

Bangalore □
Mysore

○ Pondicherry

Andaman
Islands

Almindivi
Islands

Cochin □
◆ Madurai

Trivandrum □

SRI
LANKA

N

INDIAN
OCEAN

Nicobar
Islands

KEY

cities and towns by
population

◆ over 1,000,000

□ over 500,000

○ over 100,000

● under 100,000

other symbols

▲ high points

-- country border

-- claimed by India

| 0 | 160 | 320 | 640 | 800 km |
| 0 | 100 | 200 | 400 | 500 miles |

The Ganges Plain

The state of Uttar Pradesh in the north-east is India's most populous state. Dominated by the Ganges River and containing four of Hinduism's seven holy towns, it has a population of 139 million.

The sand dunes near Sam village in the Thar Desert have been turned into a national park, and the area is now a popular destination for camel safaris.

The area immediately south of the Himalayan range is one of the most fertile areas of land in the world. It extends from Kolkata (formerly Calcutta) in the east, north to the capital Delhi, towards the Himalayan foothills and west towards the state of Rajasthan. The area is almost completely flat – Delhi is only 200 metres (650 feet) above sea level – and was formed by sediment, washed down from the emerging Himalayan range 40 million years ago. Today, the silt and debris are more than 5000 metres (16,400 feet) deep in some areas and hold some of the largest reserves of underground water in the world. Each year, rivers carry and deposit huge quantities of sand and clay, called alluvium, which renews the plain's fertility. The underground water reserves allow the land to be irrigated over a wide area. The plains sustain one of the densest concentrations of people in the world.

The deltas of West Bengal and the southern part of India's neighbour Bangladesh are only 5000 years old. They were created by huge silt deposits flowing into the Ganges River faster than the sea could remove them. As the silt deposits built up, land was created. The sediment does not reach into western India, with the result that the arid area of India's great desert, the Thar, was formed.

The Ganges River

The Ganges is more than just a river to Hindus – it is their holiest river. Every Hindu wants to make a pilgrimage to the Ganges at some point in his or her life. A fundamental Hindu belief is reincarnation – that is, the idea that when we die, we are endlessly reborn in another body, not always a human one (see page 114). Hindus believe that bathing in the river washes away the sins not only of the present life but of all previous lives. The holiest place to bathe in the Ganges is the north-eastern city of Varanasi (above), one of the world's oldest continuously inhabited cities. If Hindus are not able to bathe in the Ganges during their lifetime, they hope to have their ashes scattered in the waters at Varanasi after death. This, they believe, ends the cycle of rebirth.

Varanasi's river banks are a spectacular sight. The steps leading down to the river are known as **ghats**. There are more than 100 ghats along this stretch of the Ganges. There are ghats for bathing, praying, washing, laundry and cremation of the dead. A boat trip at dawn, as the sun rises, is the best time to see all these activities.

The Deccan Plateau

South of the Ganges Plain is the arid, high plateau known as the Deccan Plateau, which tapers down to southern India. It is bordered on each side by the Western and Eastern Ghats, ranges of hills running parallel to the coasts. The Western Ghats are higher than the Eastern Ghats and have a wider coastal strip that includes the states of Goa and Kerala. The Ghats taper south and meet towards the tip of India in the Nilgiri Hills.

The Nilgiri Hills in the south are named after the blue haze that seems to hang over the uplands. Nilgiri means 'Blue Mountains'.

The landscape of the Deccan Plateau is rocky, and the Marathas (see page 55) built impregnable fortresses on the plateau's flat tops. The surface of the Deccan Plateau has been eroded by rivers, such as the Krishna, that flow across the plateau from west to east, emptying into the Bay of Bengal. The rivers produce spectacular gorges with waterfalls that dry up during the dry season and become rushing torrents of water in the rainy **monsoon** season (see page 24). In Maharashtra state in western India are the Buddhist caves of Ajanta. Their walls are painted with **murals** that date from 200 BC to AD 650. Nearby are the later Buddhist, Hindu and Jain caves of Ellora (see page 96). Thorn forest and scrub cover the inland areas and the eastern parts of the plateau.

In contrast to the Deccan Plateau, the Nilgiri Hills are lush and fertile and are covered with spice forests, coffee bushes and tea plantations. The southern state of Tamil Nadu is known as the rice bowl of India because there are many green rice fields, called paddy fields. The western coastal states of Kerala and Goa are also green and fertile and are covered in rainforest. Kerala's distinctive landscape is dotted with coconut palms, rubber trees and canals, or backwaters, that make travelling by boat the best way to get around. Goa, north of Kerala, has rice fields and tropical fruit trees, such as mango and papaya.

Fishing nets like these at Kerala were introduced by the Chinese. It was through Kerala, historically a major trading area, that Chinese ideas and products were taken to the West.

ADMINISTRATIVE DIVISIONS

India is divided into 28 states, covering large areas of the country, and seven smaller union territories, which are either island groups or distinct city areas. Each state has a governor, whose role is mostly ceremonial, and a legislative assembly based on the national parliament with a council of ministers led by a chief minister. Below state level, administration is divided into districts, which are then divided into community-level blocks consisting of about a hundred villages.

THE STATES OF INDIA

India is divided into 28 states and seven union territories. These are listed below, with the capital of each region marked with a dot on the map on the left. Chandigarh is capital of Haryana, Punjab and the union territory of Chandigarh.

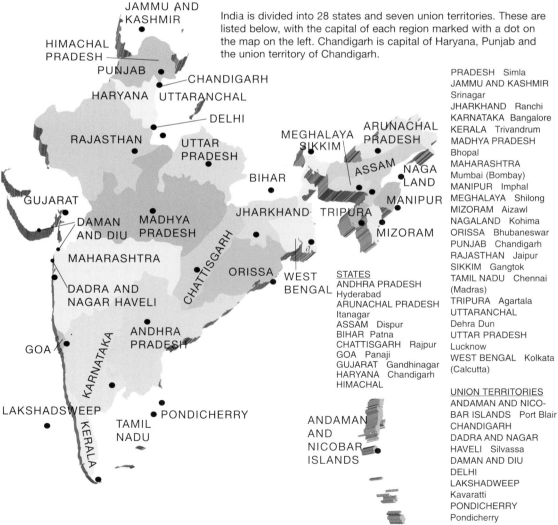

PRADESH Simla
JAMMU AND KASHMIR Srinagar
JHARKHAND Ranchi
KARNATAKA Bangalore
KERALA Trivandrum
MADHYA PRADESH Bhopal
MAHARASHTRA Mumbai (Bombay)
MANIPUR Imphal
MEGHALAYA Shilong
MIZORAM Aizawl
NAGALAND Kohima
ORISSA Bhubaneswar
PUNJAB Chandigarh
RAJASTHAN Jaipur
SIKKIM Gangtok
TAMIL NADU Chennai (Madras)
TRIPURA Agartala
UTTARANCHAL Dehra Dun
UTTAR PRADESH Lucknow
WEST BENGAL Kolkata (Calcutta)

UNION TERRITORIES
ANDAMAN AND NICO-BAR ISLANDS Port Blair
CHANDIGARH
DADRA AND NAGAR HAVELI Silvassa
DAMAN AND DIU
DELHI
LAKSHADWEEP Kavaratti
PONDICHERRY Pondicherry

STATES
ANDHRA PRADESH Hyderabad
ARUNACHAL PRADESH Itanagar
ASSAM Dispur
BIHAR Patna
CHATTISGARH Rajpur
GOA Panaji
GUJARAT Gandhinagar
HARYANA Chandigarh
HIMACHAL

INDIA'S CLIMATE

India is such a huge country that it contains many different types of climate and geographical features. It is quite possible for it to be snowing in the Himalayas while in the south, the sun beats down and temperatures can rise to more than 40 °C (104 °F). In the desert state of Rajasthan during the 1980s, no rain fell for several years, leading to drought and water rationing for the local people. In contrast, the city of Mawsynram, in Meghalaya state in north-east India, is the wettest place on Earth.

India lies in the Northern Hemisphere, and so its seasons – spring, summer, autumn and winter – occur at the same time as they do in Europe. The seasons change according to the arrival and departure of the monsoon (see box page 24). Spring falls between February and April; then temperatures rise until the heat and humidity become so stifling during the Indian summer that the monsoon rains provide a welcome relief. Once the rains finish in September or October, the temperature drops and conditions are once again more comfortable. In the capital city, Delhi, it is cool enough for people to wear sweaters in December and January, but the south stays constantly hot throughout the year.

Because the Indian peninsula is still moving northwards, thrusting under the Eurasian Plate, the area of the Himalayas and other ranges to the east are prone to earthquakes, and landslides are common.

Kolkata experiences constant temperatures throughout the year and extremes of rainfall, while in Delhi temperatures drop significantly in winter.

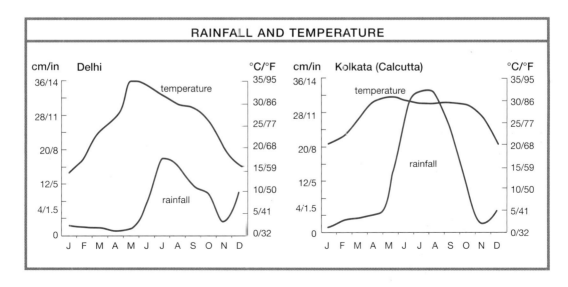

RAINFALL AND TEMPERATURE

The monsoon

The word 'monsoon' is Arabic for 'season'. It describes the rains that arrive in India each year between June and October. The monsoon is caused by the wind changing direction. The north-easterly winds that normally sweep across India bringing dry air from Central Asia are replaced by wet and warm south-westerly winds.

The Indian monsoon is unique because of its regularity and the amount of moisture that passes over the country. During the monsoon, it usually rains every day. By the end of September, dry, brown-baked land has turned green and lush, although most of the monsoon rains run straight into the sea. The monsoon clouds have an average depth of 6000 m (19,685 ft) compared to only 2000 m (6560 ft) during the summer rains in Japan. The rains decrease the further north the monsoon travels, particularly towards the north-west, which remains comparatively dry.

The southern state of Tamil Nadu does not receive its rains during the summer monsoon. Instead, the retreating monsoon, now blowing from the north-east, brings heavy rains between the months of October and December.

There are many myths about the Indian monsoon. One is that it always arrives on 1 June in Thiruvananthapuram, the largest southern-most city. In fact the monsoon can arrive at any date. When the monsoon fails to arrive, serious consequences follow, such as the drought that hit Rajasthan in the 1980s.

ANIMALS AND PLANTS

India is home to unique species of plants and animals that are some of the most spectacular in the world. There are more than 500 species of mammals in India, more than 2000 species of birds and 30,000 species of insects. Animals are part of Indian daily life. Two of the most popular gods in the Hindu religion are the monkey god, Hanuman, and the elephant god, Ganesh.

In India's cities, cows, considered sacred by the Hindus, wander freely in the streets amid the buses and taxis. In the countryside, the black-faced langur monkey, with its long tail, and the rhesus macaque monkey, with its orange-red behind, play in trees next to villages. Animals are never far away in India, largely because people have moved into the animals' habitat and the limited space has forced humans and animals to live side by side.

The destruction of the natural habitat has started to have disastrous consequences for India's animals. The Indian elephant, the tiger and the Asiatic lion are still found in India today, but poaching and the growing human population threaten the survival of many species. Some animals, such as the cheetah, are already extinct in India.

Holy cows

Cows have been worshipped in India since ancient times. The cow represents nurturing and fertility. It is linked to the mother goddess and is a symbol of Mother India itself. The sacred cow is the deity Khamdenu, and cow dung and urine are used in India to purify the home (the urine wards off insects). Each part of the cow's body is seen as significant. The horns symbolize the gods, the face the Sun and Moon, the shoulders Agni (the god of fire) and the legs the Himalayas.

National parks and Project Tiger

India recognized the threat to its wildlife in the 1970s and began creating national parks to preserve the natural world. Today, there are almost 70 national parks and 330 sanctuaries spread across India.

Tigers once roamed across the whole of India. At the start of the 20th century, the estimated tiger population was 40,000. When the British ruled India (see page 58),

The tiger is India's national animal, and the country is unique in having both lions and tigers. Conservationists argue that the amount India spends on wildlife (equivalent to 0.2 per cent of its GDP) should be increased because the country is so important ecologically.

tiger hunts were a popular sport for the British and wealthy Indians. One hundred tigers a day could be killed. Today, it is estimated that there are only 7000 tigers left in the world, of which half are in India.

Project Tiger was started by the Indian government and the World Wildlife Fund to encourage the tiger to breed by giving it protected areas of wilderness. In 1973, 25,000 square kilometres (9650 square miles) was set aside for Project Tiger. There were early successes, and the number of tigers increased from a low of 1800 in the 1970s to 3500 in the 1990s. However, the tiger is again under threat from ruthless poachers who kill the animal to sell its skin and body parts to the Chinese medicine market.

The national parks are home to many other species of animals in addition to the tiger. The Asiatic lion, which is found only in the Gir National

NATIONAL PARKS

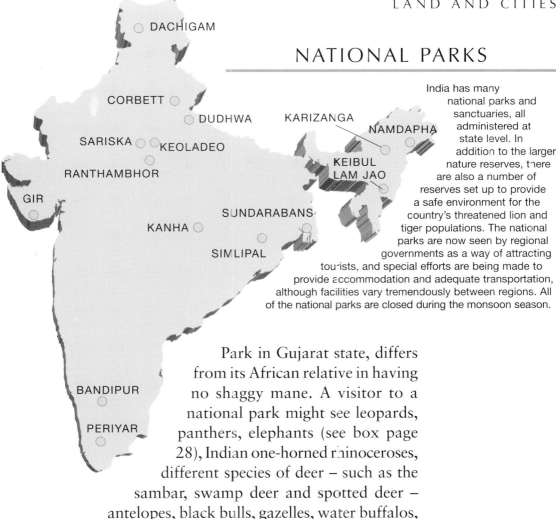

DACHIGAM

CORBETT

DUDHWA   KARIZANGA

NAMDAPHA

SARISKA   KEOLADEO

KEIBUL
LAM JAO

RANTHAMBHOR

GIR

SUNDARABANS

KANHA

SIMLIPAL

BANDIPUR

PERIYAR

India has many national parks and sanctuaries, all administered at state level. In addition to the larger nature reserves, there are also a number of reserves set up to provide a safe environment for the country's threatened lion and tiger populations. The national parks are now seen by regional governments as a way of attracting tourists, and special efforts are being made to provide accommodation and adequate transportation, although facilities vary tremendously between regions. All of the national parks are closed during the monsoon season.

Park in Gujarat state, differs from its African relative in having no shaggy mane. A visitor to a national park might see leopards, panthers, elephants (see box page 28), Indian one-horned rhinoceroses, different species of deer – such as the sambar, swamp deer and spotted deer – antelopes, black bulls, gazelles, water buffalos, bison and, in the Himalayas, yaks.

In the countryside, jackals and hyenas scavenge, and birds such as vultures and crows sit in the branches of trees. The Gangetic dolphin swims in the Ganges River, and the sloth bear, with its long snout, lives in forests. Sloth bears are often caught and used by street entertainers, who earn money from the bears' 'dancing'.

India has a huge variety of birdlife that varies according to the climate. Doves, crows and vultures are a common sight in Indian cities. In the swamps of India, cormorants, cranes and storks are to be found. The most common and perhaps prettiest waterbird is the kingfisher, which has an orange breast and bright blue upper body. Birds such as

The Indian elephant

The Indian elephant is smaller than its African relative, and is the second-largest land mammal after the African elephant. Its ears are smaller and the female is tuskless. Sometimes even the male Indian elephant does not have tusks. The Indian elephant is revered in the Hindu religion and is valued for its hard work in daily life. It is not unusual to see an elephant at work in rural areas, carrying goods with its trunk or dragging logs. The elephant has been used by people for about 5000 years, and each working elephant has a keeper, called a *mahout*, who looks after the animal. Looking after an elephant can be hard work – a working elephant needs to be fed for about eighteen hours a day by hand. It eats between 100 and 300 kg (220 and 660 lb) of vegetation every day. Wild elephants can be dangerous if they come into contact with humans. They often destroy buildings and crops.

India has over 2000 species of fish. Sharks are found in the country's coastal waters and even venture inland along some of the major rivers.

the egret, mina and parakeet live in the grasslands, while at higher altitudes are magpies, wagtails and pheasants.

India is also home to many types of reptiles, including large snakes such as the Indian rock python and the king cobra. In houses all over India, the gecko, a small lizard, is a frequent visitor and comes out at night to catch insects. Crocodiles live in some of the country's rivers. The most common of these fearsome reptiles are the mugger (or marsh) crocodiles and the gharial, which live in fresh water. The gharial is between 6 and 8 metres (19 and 26 feet) long, twice the size of the mugger.

Among India's most distinctive features are its colourful flowers and trees. Flamboyant bougainvillaea trees are seen all over the country with their bright orange, pink and purple leaves. The frangipani bush's white flowers have a sweet scent and are also very common, as is the colourful hibiscus plant with its trumpet-shaped flowers that vary from scarlet to yellow. Imported from Brazil, the jacaranda tree with its blue-purple flowers lines town and country roads, as does the yellow-and-red-flowered tamarind tree. Coconut palm trees and fruit trees grow all over the south and coastal parts of India.

In the Himalayas, alpine flowers and trees such as pine, spruce and fir are commonly found. The most famous tree in India is the banyan – the Indian fig tree. It is planted by temples, in villages and alongside roads. Another typical Indian tree – the bodhi – owes its fame to the Buddha (see page 114), who is said to have reached enlightenment (religious wisdom) beneath its branches.

The banyan tree spreads by aerial roots that hang down from its branches. These reach down to the ground to form new trunks, so that one tree may eventually appear to be a dense thicket of trunks.

After 1947, millions of Hindu refugees from Pakistan were housed in 'model towns', huge developments on the edge of the larger cities. Typically these had five-storey apartment blocks with facilities attached.

INDIA'S CITIES

Although India is predominantly a rural country – 75 per cent of the population live in the countryside – almost 250 million people live in India's cities. The major cities all continue to grow rapidly as people from the countryside flock to them daily in search of work. Despite being the capital city, Delhi does not have the largest population – both Mumbai (Bombay) and Kolkata (Calcutta) are larger. People living on the streets is a common sight in every major city, and **shanty towns** – shacks built of discarded materials – house thousands in every city. Some smaller cities, such as the southern city of Bangalore, grew very rapidly at the end of the 20th century. The immigrants to Bangalore are mostly highly educated university graduates who work in the computer technology field.

A view of the city of Mumbai with the docks in the background.

Mumbai

The city of Mumbai used to be called Bombay. It lies on India's west coast and is India's largest city with a population of over 15 million. It is also the country's financial

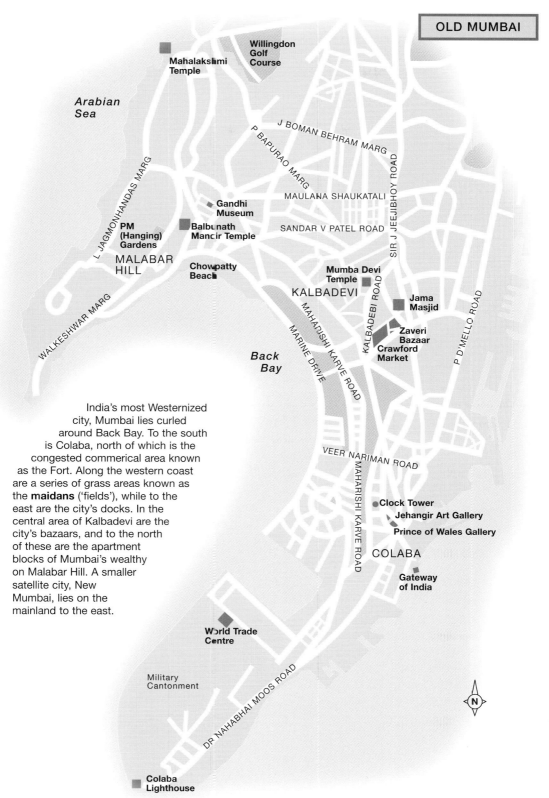

OLD MUMBAI

Arabian Sea

Mahalakshmi Temple

Willingdon Golf Course

J BOMAN BEHRAM MARG

P BAPURAO MARG

MAULANA SHAUKATALI

SANDAR V PATEL ROAD

SIR J JEEJIBHOY ROAD

L JAGMONHANDAS MARG

Gandhi Museum

PM (Hanging) Gardens

Balbunath Mancir Temple

MALABAR HILL

Chowpatty Beach

Mumba Devi Temple

KALBADEVI

KALBADEBI ROAD

Jama Masjid

Zaveri Bazaar

Crawford Market

P D'MELLO ROAD

WALKESHWAR MARG

MAHARISHI KARVE ROAD

MARINE DRIVE

Back Bay

India's most Westernized city, Mumbai lies curled around Back Bay. To the south is Colaba, north of which is the congested commerical area known as the Fort. Along the western coast are a series of grass areas known as the **maidans** ('fields'), while to the east are the city's docks. In the central area of Kalbadevi are the city's bazaars, and to the north of these are the apartment blocks of Mumbai's wealthy on Malabar Hill. A smaller satellite city, New Mumbai, lies on the mainland to the east.

VEER NARIMAN ROAD

MAHARISHI KARVE ROAD

Clock Tower

Jehangir Art Gallery

Prince of Wales Gallery

COLABA

Gateway of India

World Trade Centre

Military Cantonment

DR NAHABHAI MOOS ROAD

N

Colaba Lighthouse

Dhaba wallahs

One of Mumbai's unique features is the dhaba wallahs. Each day at around midday, the dhaba wallahs gather at the suburban rail stations. They are waiting for the arrival of thousands of tiffin (or lunch) boxes, which they then deliver to individual office workers.

The system works like this – in the suburbs, a worker's wife prepares his daily lunch of rice, vegetables and dhal (lentil curry) and packs it into the heat-retaining metal tiffin boxes. The boxes are then transported by train to Mumbai where the dhaba wallahs collect them and distribute them. It is unusual for a tiffin box to get lost or be late because a simple colour-coded system tells the illiterate dhaba wallahs where to distribute and then collect the lunch boxes, which are later transported back to the suburbs.

and commercial centre and home to one of India's biggest industries – films. This industry is known as 'Bollywood'. The film industry attracts many aspiring actors to the city, who come in the hope of superstardom.

Like New York City's Manhattan, Mumbai is an island, attached to the mainland by numerous bridges. Mumbai was created from seven islands made into one through land reclamation. The island is no more than 5 kilometres (3 miles) wide and 22 kilometres (14 miles) long at any one point. It is bordered on three sides by the Arabian Sea. Into this small area are squeezed many of the city's inhabitants, its industries, docks, warehouses and major businesses. The city is expanding rapidly, and part of the mainland forms the greater Mumbai suburbs. Mumbai has the largest shanty town in Asia, called Dharvi, which is home to approximately 1 million people.

Known as 'tin towns' because of the flimsy shacks' corrugated tin roofs, they have inadequate sewerage, limited running water and no paved footpaths. They are home to illiterate manual workers from the countryside.

Mumbai has some of the highest rent prices anywhere in the world, and for many, even a shanty home is unaffordable. For years, whole families lived on central Mumbai's streets – cooking, sleeping and eating in the open – but recent efforts to clean up the city have resulted in these families being moved out of the city centre.

In a city where money is so important, one of its most enjoyable places is free. As dusk falls, families gather on Chowpatty Beach to walk, sit or enjoy a snack from one of the many *bhelpuri* vendors on the beach. *Bhelpuri* is made of noodles, puffed rice and wheat crackers mixed with diced boiled potatoes (see page 110). Fortune-tellers, masseurs, monkey trainers, hand-operated Ferris wheels and food-sellers are all found on the beach.

Mumbai life moves at a fast pace. The streets are choked with cars, black-and-yellow taxis, double-decker buses, scooters, auto-rickshaws and even the odd cow. Office workers pour in and out of the city's railway stations. Between 2 and 3 million workers travel to the city each day. Many commute for up to two hours a day on overcrowded trains because they cannot afford the high rents of the city centre.

Mumbai's Chowpatty Beach is a long, semi-circular-shaped beach on the Arabian Sea. At night the bay is all lit up. From the top of nearby Malabar Hill it looks like a necklace of lights – hence its nickname, the 'queen's necklace'.

Delhi

India's governmental and administrative capital is Delhi. The difference between Mumbai and Delhi is equivalent to that between New York and Washington, DC, in the USA. That is, although Delhi is the capital, it is not the largest city in India and neither is it the financial and commercial centre. With 9 million inhabitants, Delhi is India's third-largest city.

What is now modern Delhi has been the site of more than a dozen cities from around the 9th century BC. Present-day Delhi consists of two parts: Old Delhi, which was the capital under the Mughals (see page 52) between the 17th and 19th centuries, and New Delhi, which was created by the British when they decided to move the capital from Kolkata (Calcutta) in 1911. New Delhi is distinguished from other Indian cities by its broad avenues and green spaces, although the sense of space is being diminished as the population expands rapidly. Old Delhi, in contrast, is more like other Indian cities with its narrow streets and bustling activity.

The Indian flag flies above the battlements of Delhi's Red Fort. The fort was built over ten years, from 1638 to 1648, the period of the greatest Mughal power in the region.

Old Delhi lies to the north of the city, and is dominated by the Red Fort, the massive center of Mughal government completed in 1648, and by the Jami Masjid, India's largest mosque. Off Chandni Chowk run Delhi's bazaars, selling everything from spices to silver and from car parts to chickens. South of the bazaars lies New Delhi. Since 1931 the center of India's national government, New Delhi's tree-lined avenues contrast sharply with the bustle to the north. Southern Delhi, a rapidly expanding suburban area, contains the remains of several of Delhi's ancient cities.

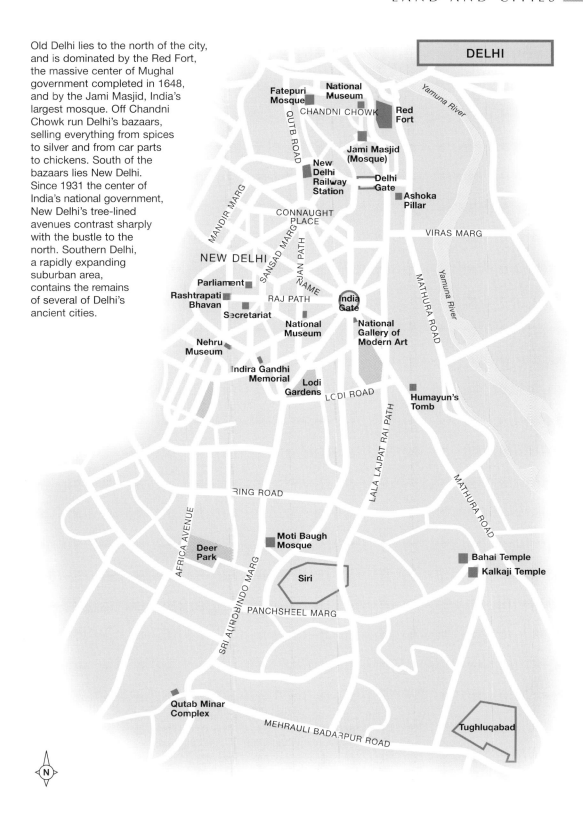

DELHI

Fatepuri Mosque
National Museum
CHANDNI CHOWK
Red Fort
Yamuna River
QUTB ROAD
Jami Masjid (Mosque)
New Delhi Railway Station
Delhi Gate
Ashoka Pillar
MANDIR MARG
CONNAUGHT PLACE
VIRAS MARG
NEW DELHI
SANSAD MARG
JAN PATH
NAME
MATHURA ROAD
Yamuna River
Parliament
Rashtrapati Bhavan
RAJ PATH
India Gate
Secretariat
National Museum
National Gallery of Modern Art
Nehru Museum
Indira Gandhi Memorial
Lodi Gardens
LODI ROAD
LALA LAJPAT RAI PATH
Humayun's Tomb
RING ROAD
AFRICA AVENUE
Moti Baugh Mosque
Deer Park
SRI AUROBINDO MARG
Siri
Bahai Temple
Kalkaji Temple
PANCHSHEEL MARG
Qutab Minar Complex
MEHRAULI BADARPUR ROAD
Tughluqabad
MATHURA ROAD

N

Delhi has always played an important part in India's history. Its northerly position gave it strategic importance because India's numerous invaders entered the country from the north. An old saying is that whoever founds a new city at Delhi will eventually lose control of it, and the saying has been proved right each time. Today, Delhi is one of India's fastest-growing cities as rural workers flock to it in search of work.

Old Delhi was laid out by Emperor Shah Jahan in about 1640 as a walled city. Shah Jahan was a Mughal ruler who reigned from 1627 to 1658. Naturally enough, Old Delhi contains many of the oldest streets, buildings and monuments in Delhi. The Lal Qila, or Red Fort, is a massive, red sandstone fort containing palaces and halls. It was the seat of the Mughal emperors (see page 52) and once contained the fabulous solid gold, jewel-encrusted Peacock Throne. Facing the fort is

The symbol of the swastika – which is more famous in Europe and the USA for its use by the German Nazis – was originally an ancient Aryan symbol of perfection. Many Hindu temples include the symbol in their design.

Delhi's seven cities

The importance of Delhi in northern India is borne out by the several ancient cities founded in and around the present capital. The earliest of these was built to the south-west of modern Delhi in AD 736 and named Lal Kot by its Tomara Rajput founders. It was captured by a rival clan in 1180 and given its present name of Qila Rai Pithora. In 1290, the Turkish Khaljis came to power, establishing the second city of Siri to the east in 1303, which rapidly became a thriving commercial centre. Another fortress was built to the east of the original city a few years later, but was swiftly abandoned because of a lack of water. In 1327 a fourth city, Jahanpanah, was built between Lal Kot and Siri and a fifth, Firozabad, was built in 1354. It was not until the 16th century that the sixth city, the fort of Din-Panah (now known as Purana Qila), was built by the Afghan king Sher Shah, who had driven out the ruling sultan Humayun; the latter reclaimed the city in 1555. The seventh city, the magnificent new walled capital of Shajahanabad, was built by Shah Jahan in the 17th century. Parts of this complex, encompassing the Red Fort and the Jama Masjid, or Friday Mosque, is now known as Old Delhi. Only with the building of the planned city of New Delhi were Delhi's earlier cities finally joined into one vast urban centre.

the ancient bazaar, or marketplace, of Chandni Chowk with its narrow maze of crowded alleys running off the main street. Chandni Chowk bustles with shops selling gold, spices, clothes and many other goods. The best way to explore Chandni Chowk is by rickshaw, which can be hired very cheaply.

Less than 2 kilometres (1 mile) from the Red Fort is the Jama Masjid, or Friday Mosque, which was the last great architectural work of Shah Jahan. A **mosque** is a place of worship for Muslims. This is the largest example in India, and as many as 20,000 Muslims can pray there at one time. Together with the Red Fort, it dominates the skyline of Old Delhi.

Delhi's bustling Chandni Chowk was once a tree-lined canal. Today it is Old Delhi's main thoroughfare.

Trams, cars, taxis and auto-rickshaws choke the streets in central Kolkata.

Kolkata

Kolkata, formerly known as Calcutta, is India's second-largest city with a population of 14 million. Kolkata lies on the east coast in the state of Bengal. Compared to India's other major cities, Kolkata is relatively young. It was created 300 years ago by British traders so that their company, the East India Company, could have a port to export its goods. Once the British took political control of India, Kolkata became the capital. With its cathedral, buildings dedicated to Queen Victoria – who was Empress of India from 1876 to 1901 – and colonial architecture, Kolkata resembles a British city more than an Indian one.

The Black Hole of Calcutta

In 1756 the new ruler of Bengal, the young nawab (or prince) Siraj-ud-daula, was eager to seize British-owned gold. He easily captured Calcutta from the British, and all but 146 of the British residents fled. Those who remained were captured and locked overnight in an underground cell with only one tiny window. The outside temperature was over 40 °C (104 °F). Next morning when the warders unlocked the door, they found 123 men and women had suffocated to death. The British called the incident the 'Black Hole of Calcutta'.

It is the only Indian city to have an underground railway, which opened in 1984.

The centre of Kolkata is clustered around the Maidan, one of the largest city parks in the world. Planned at the same time as the military base of Fort William in the 18th century, Maidan contrasts sharply with the overcrowded streets that border it, particularly to the north. On the west bank of the Hooghly River lies the industrial area of Howrah, while the south of the city is largely residential.

Kolkata suffers from a bad image. Many outsiders consider the city of Kolkata to be poor, squalid and dirty. The charity worker Mother Teresa, who founded her Sisters of Mercy mission to help the poorest people of Kolkata, did so because she saw the most poverty and deprivation in and around the city. While Kolkata's problems are huge, the city is also dynamic and vibrant and is home to many of India's artists and intellectuals. The city has a thriving Bengali theatre scene, large Indian classical music festivals and many art galleries.

KOLKATA

Digambar Jain Temple

BELGACHIA ROAD

N. GHAT STREET

Sitalnath Jain Temple

HOWRAH BRIDGE

Rabindra Bharati

Marble Palace

KESHAR CHANDRA SEN STREET

STRAND ROAD

Hooghly River

Nakhoda Mosque

COLLEGE STREET

Government House

LENIN SARANI

Fort William

CHOWRINGHEE

New Market

Indian Museum

A J C BOSE ROAD

The Maidan

KINDERPORE ROAD

St Paul's Cathedral

A J C BOSE ROAD

National Library

ASHUTOSH MUKHERJEE ROAD

SARAT BOSE ROAD

ASHUTOSH CHOWDHURYROAD

Kalighat Temple

Rabrindra Sarobar (The Lakes)

N

Chennai

Chennai, formerly known as Madras, is India's fourth-largest city. With a population of nearly 6 million, Chennai is the largest city in south India. Located on India's east coast in the state of Tamil Nadu, it differs from the other major cities in its slower pace of life compared to its northerly counterparts. It was founded by the British East India Company in 1639 on a narrow 5-kilometre (3-mile) strip of land between the Kuvam (Cooum) and Adyar rivers. Chennai rose to importance as a trading post for the British in the 17th century. Repeatedly attacked by the French during the 18th century, the city was gradually fortified by the British. Its mixture of colonial British buildings and a strong Tamil identity give it a unique quality. The town was renamed Chennai in 1997 to reassert its precolonial identity. The city is a centre for Dravidian nationalism, a movement that represents the concerns of the native people of southern India and defends them against the cultural influence of the north and the remnants of India's colonial past.

The bulbous white domes and sandstone towers of the High Court Building at Chennai show strong Islamic influences, despite being built during the colonial period.

Chennai is divided into three main areas. The northern district consists of the original British settlement, based around George Town, a centre for banks, offices and shipping companies. In the centre of the city is the main commercial and residential area, bisected by the main thorough-fare, Anna Salai, and bordered to the east by the 5-kilometre (3-mile) marina. To the south lies Myla-pore, a major settlement since ancient times and the site of the 19th-century San Thome Cath-edral, built over the tomb of St Thomas, and the Kapalishvara Temple, dedicated to Shiva and built during the 16th century. During the 1990s, Chennai boomed as India opened up to foreign investment. The dis-advantage of this is that the previously tranquil city has become overcrowded with people who have moved from the countryside to the city to look for work.

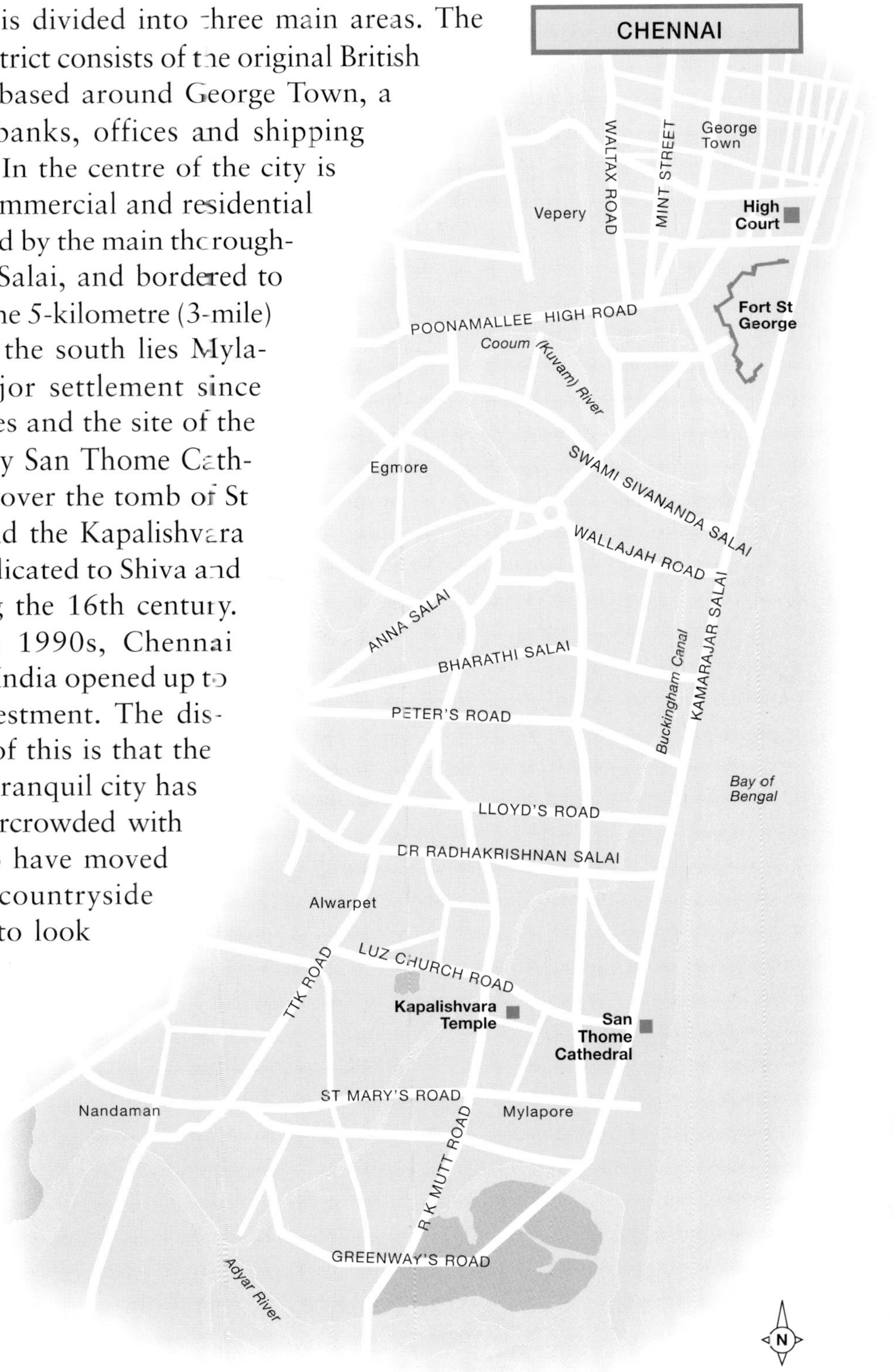

CHENNAI

George Town

WALTAX ROAD

MINT STREET

Vepery

High Court

POONAMALLEE HIGH ROAD

Cooum (Kuvam) River

Fort St George

Egmore

SWAMI SIVANANDA SALAI

WALLAJAH ROAD

KAMARAJAR SALAI

ANNA SALAI

BHARATHI SALAI

PETER'S ROAD

Buckingham Canal

Bay of Bengal

LLOYD'S ROAD

DR RADHAKRISHNAN SALAI

Alwarpet

TTK ROAD

LUZ CHURCH ROAD

Kapalishvara Temple

San Thome Cathedral

ST MARY'S ROAD

Nandaman

R K MUTT ROAD

Mylapore

Adyar River

GREENWAY'S ROAD

N

Past and Present

'India is the cradle of the human race, the birthplace of human speech, the mother of history, the grandmother of legend, and the great-grandmother of tradition.'

American writer Mark Twain

India has one of the world's oldest civilizations. Historians have found evidence of early human civilization in north India dating back to 2500 BC.

Among India's first invaders were the Aryans, who pushed India's original inhabitants, the Dravidians, southwards. Early **Hinduism** developed under the Aryans. Later the Mauryans, who were native to India, ruled over an empire that extended over a large part of the Indian subcontinent. In about 500 BC, the religion of Buddhism was born in India. The Gupta empire emerged in the 4th century AD, and brought with it many new developments in the arts and sciences. Different groups of **Muslim** invaders arrived in India after the 8th century, the most notable of which were the Mughals, who arrived in India in the 16th century. The Mughal empire saw a flowering of the arts and literature in India, and construction of some of India's most impressive buildings.

The Portuguese were the first Europeans to colonize parts of India, followed by the French, Dutch, Danish and British. In the 19th century, the British set about making India part of their empire, and by the middle of the century the British government took overall control of India. For the next 90 years or so, India was part of the British empire and did not gain its independence until 1947. Modern India is a rich mixture of traditional cultures with elements of its different foreign occupiers.

European traders are shown fighting over the spoils of Indian trade. India was the richest country on Earth until the arrival of the British in the 17th century.

FACT FILE

- India's history of civilization stretches back more than 4500 years.

- The period of the Guptas (AD 320–550) to the reign of Harsha Vardhana (AD 606–57), during which northern Indian was unified, is known as the Classical Age of Indian history.

- The era of the Gupta empire (*see* page 49) produced six systems of philosophy – Nyaya, Waissheshika, Sankhya, Yoga, Mimamsa and Vedanta. Vedanta is still the basis of Indian philosophy.

- Kerala was the first state in the world to elect a **communist** government democratically (in 1957).

EARLY CIVILIZATIONS

The seal below in the form of an ox comes from the site at Mohenjodaro in modern-day Pakistan. It was produced during the Indus civilization, which encompassed parts of northern India and lasted from about 2500 to about 1800 BC.

In the 1920s, archaeologists discovered evidence of a developed civilization in India that flourished in about 2500 BC. Archaeological excavations proved that the civilization extended across north-western and western India (the states of Gujarat and Rajasthan) and the Indus River valley (in present-day Pakistan). Known as the **Harappa** civilization, its great cities were Harappa and Mohenjodaro, both in present-day Pakistan. Archaeologists uncovered evidence of streets planned on a grid system, a sewage system, zoned housing for different social groups and public buildings. The people of the Harappa culture developed their own written

script, based on pictures, although historians still have to decipher all of the script. The people also worked with metals such as copper, bronze, lead and tin and made their own bricks in kilns.

The present-day religion of Hinduism has its origins in the religious beliefs of the Harappans. They worshipped male and female gods that are prehistoric versions of Kali, the goddess of destruction, and Siva, the god of both creation and destruction. The Harappa society was ruled by priests rather than kings. This was later reflected in the Hindu **caste** system (see page 114), where priests were the most respected members of society.

The Harappa civilization lasted for about 1000 years. Historians do not know precisely why it declined, although it is possible that repeated flooding of the towns

The Indus Civilization

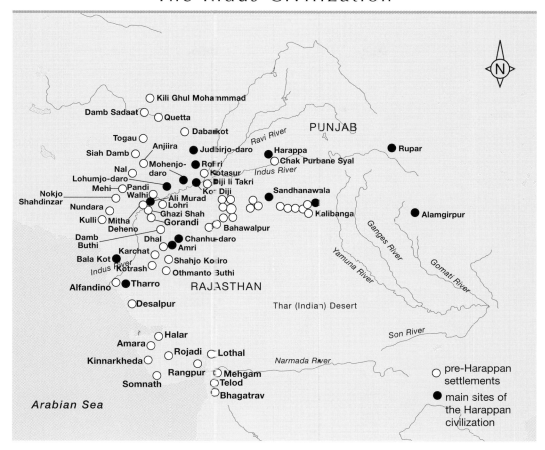

located on the banks of the Indus River and the spread of desert land and droughts contributed to its collapse. By the time the Aryans arrived from the present-day Middle East in 1500 BC, Harappan culture had all but died out.

The Aryan civilization

The Aryan people invaded India from Central Asia and moved south between 1500 and 200 BC. Although the Ayrans pushed the Dravidians – India's original inhabitants – south, the Aryans never controlled south India, which developed separately from north India. Many of the elements of modern-day India have their roots in Aryan civilization. For example, the **Sanskrit** language, the caste system, a village-based agricultural society and

The Harappan civilization developed in a relatively small area around the Indus River and was protected from attacks by desert and high mountains.

45

The Vedic Scriptures

The **Vedic** Scriptures form the basis of the Hindu religion. They were written between 1500 and 1200 BC. *Veda* means 'divine knowledge'. The four *Vedas* – *Rigveda*, *Yajurveda*, *Samaveda* and *Atharvaveda* – are a collection of hymns and religious texts. They were composed as hymns, or religious homages, to the magnificent Himalayan Mountains, the lush river valleys, the green forests of ancient India and the divine power that created such beauty. Although the Aryans worshipped many gods, the *Vedas* reveal that the Aryans believed all the gods to be manifestations, or appearances, of one divine power. This idea underlies contemporary Hindu belief (see page 113).

the origins of the Hindu religion all date from this period. The Aryans were the first invaders to build their capital at Delhi.

The Aryans worked as farmers and raised cattle. The people whose land they had invaded were made to work in the fields, ploughing the land with oxen and cultivating crops such as barley, cucumber and sugarcane. The Aryans became wealthy through their farming and through the use of slave labour. With plenty of free time, they turned their attentions to pursuing philosophical questions. The search for answers about the human position in the universe was linked to the Ayrans' religious worship of gods of nature. That is, the Aryans believed that humans were part of nature and that all nature was divine. They developed a sophisticated spoken language, Sanskrit, but were slow to develop writing. Instead, they passed on information orally.

The Aryans were organized into tribes, each with an hereditary chief. The tribes were then divided along caste lines. 'Caste' was the name given to the grouping of Hindu society into four main divisions. Originally, the division was based on colour, with the fair-skinned Aryans favoured over the dark-skinned Dravidian slaves. This was called the *varna* (colour) division. The Aryans then were subdivided into the following groups, or castes, according to their occupation: the **Brahmins** (priests), *Kshatriyas* (warriors), *Vaishyas* (farmers) and *Shudras* (menial workers). At first the divisions were flexible, and it was possible for people to move from one group to another. Later, a person's caste position was determined at birth and changing from one caste to another became difficult. The caste system continues to exist today (see page 114).

While the Aryans continued to hold power in the north, invaders arrived in other parts of India, including Greece's Alexander the Great (356–323 BC). He reached western India in 326 BC, but his troops refused to march further than the Beas River, the most easterly point in the Persian empire that Alexander had conquered. He and his troops turned back without increasing his empire by conquering India.

The Mauryan empire

Two centuries before Alexander reached India, an Indian empire had started to develop in the north. The Mauryan empire expanded from its capital in present-day Patna, in Bihar state. India's size, and the fact that the Aryans controlled only part of it, meant it was inevitable that other groups would seize power and expand wherever possible. The Mauryans extended their territory into lands in the west left vacant by Alexander's departure. The Mauryan empire controlled northern India from its capital from 321 BC until 184 BC.

The Mauryans were the first native Indians to unify much of India. Those who held power formed an extensive bureaucracy that collected taxes efficiently from the

The Mauryan empire, named after the ruler Chandragupta Maurya, became the first Indian empire and marked the first unification of the north of the country.

The Mauryan empire

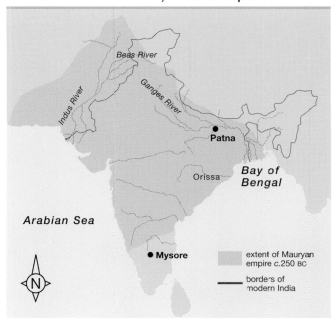

agriculture-based society. The Mauryan rulers used slaves, labourers and prisoners to work on their huge farms, while private landowners used paid labourers to till their land. Another source of revenue was the gambling houses. The empire reached its peak under the leadership of the emperor Asoka (see box below), who was a successful and inspirational leader of his people.

Emperor Asoka

When Asoka (died *c.*232 BC) inherited his empire in 272 BC, it covered the entire Indian subcontinent with the exception of present-day Orissa. The empire stretched from today's Afghanistan to Assam in the east, and from the Himalayas in the north to Mysore in the south. Shocked by the dead bodies that littered the battlefield after he conquered Orissa, which he had quickly captured, Asoka turned his back on warfare. He became a pacifist (a person who is against warfare) and converted to the relatively new religion of Buddhism.

Buddhism emerged in India about 500 BC (see page 114). This new religion rejected the *Vedas* and the caste system of Hinduism. Buddhism teaches that the path to salvation – the goal of every Buddhist – comes by reaching 'enlightenment'. Enlightenment is a state anybody can reach once they decide no longer to desire worldly things, such as wealth, and to learn moderation in all things. Unlike Hinduism, Buddhism teaches that a person's destiny, or fate, is not predetermined but can be directed by the person.

Asoka made Buddhism the official religion of his empire. In a series of edicts, or public notices, he urged his subjects to follow the code of **dharma** – morality, piety, virtue and social order. The edicts were inscribed on columns and rocks across the empire, some of which survive today. The lion pillar of Asoka is the official emblem of the Republic of India and is found on every rupee note and coin. Following Asoka's death in 232 BC, the Mauryan empire started to fall apart and by 184 BC had collapsed completely.

The south

Events in north India often had little bearing on the south. While Buddhism and, to a lesser extent, the religion of Jainism (see page 115) overtook Hinduism in the north, the south continued to be a Hindu stronghold. The area had developed trading links with the Egyptian, Roman and Greek empires. It also traded with South-East Asia and China. Reports of the battles of the warring kings of the Chera, Chola and ancient Pandya kingdoms in the south formed the basis of a distinctive south Indian literature. Known as Sangam literature, it consisted of poems composed by groups of travelling poets, or minstrels. One assembly of these travelling musicians saw more than 2000 poems being composed collectively at one time.

The subjugation of the Shakas in Gujarat in western India secured the trade of the western coast and made Gupta India the centre of a vast trading network, stretching from China to Europe.

The Gupta empire

Following the collapse of the Mauryan empire, a period of confusion followed as rival kingdoms rose and fell. The Gupta empire emerged in the 4th century AD and brought with it a period of stability and a flourishing of the arts and sciences. Over the next two centuries, the boundaries of the empire changed under different rulers, but the period was mostly peaceful. The Buddhist monastery at Ajanta (see page 92), with its magnificent **murals**, or wall paintings, was built

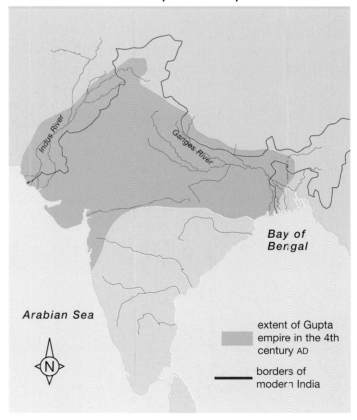

The Gupta empire

Indus River

Ganges River

Bay of Bengal

Arabian Sea

N

extent of Gupta empire in the 4th century AD

borders of modern India

in the 5th century. In the field of science, the astronomer Aryabhatta put forward the theory that the Earth moved around the Sun. We now know that this theory is correct, although it was ignored at that time. He also calculated the time it takes for the Earth to revolve around the Sun to 365.3586805 days, which was amazingly accurate given that there were no telescopes, computers or calculators at the time. It was not until about 1000 years later that the same theory was proposed in Europe, by Copernicus (AD 1473–1543). His theory, too, was opposed at the time. In literature, through his use of images and his choice of words, the writer Kalidasa took the Sanskrit language to new poetic heights. The Gupta age also saw the Hindu caste system become more established, as did the idea that women's position in society should be inferior to men's.

By the end of the 6th century AD, the Gupta empire had collapsed, and the last great Hindu empire of the north was at an end. Smaller kingdoms tried to gain power, and groups from the north-west started to invade. The next few centuries saw different groups seize power. Among these groups were the Rajputs who, from the 7th century AD, became a major power in north-western India. The Rajputs of Rajasthan were a warrior race. Independent centres of Rajput power sprang up, but the Rajputs were never strong enough to take over-all control. The intricately carved temples of Khajuraho, in north-east India, date from the Rajput dynasty of the Chandelas (AD 916–1203).

> The south of India achieved great wealth through its trade with other civilizations. These included both the Egyptians and the Romans, who bought spices, ivory and silk from the Indians in return for gold.

The first Muslims in India

Initial incursions by Muslim Arabs into India were relatively peaceful. The Arab troops of Mohammed ibn al Qasim allowed Hindus to continue practising their religion. This changed with the invasions of the Turkish commander Mahmud of Ghazna (Ghazna included modern Afghanistan and Iran). Between AD 1000 and 1027, he made seventeen raids into India, looting Hindu temples and massacring the inhabitants.

This began a period of Muslim attacks on India, from the Persian Mamluk dynasty, then came the Khaljis and finally the Tugluqs. By the time that Tamerlane the Great's incursions into India in 1398 (see opposite) brought about the break-up of the Arabian sultanate (the empire that ruled part of India), Muslim influence had been firmly established in northern India.

MUSLIM INVADERS

Successive Muslim invaders from Central Asia swept into India – the Turks, the Afghans and the Mongol leader Timur, or Tamerlane, plundered the northern plains. Until the arrival of the Muslim Mughals in the 16th century, and their subsequent domination of India, power shifted between Muslim invaders and the resident Hindus. The Hindus were often at a disadvantage because local rivalries stopped them from forming a unified defence. In addition, the Hindu caste system allowed only the warrior caste, the *Kshatriyas*, to fight in battle, thereby limiting the number of available men. Hindu foot soldiers and elephant-mounted soldiers were no match for the quicker Muslim invaders' archers on horseback. The boundaries of the successive Hindu kingdoms grew and shrank.

The Qutab Minar is a 73-metre (239-foot) victory tower, built in 1193 to celebrate the Muslim victory over the last Hindu kingdom in Delhi.

The Delhi Sultanate was established in AD 1206. A sultan was a type of Muslim ruler, and the land that he controlled was called a sultanate. Whereas previous invaders had been content to compromise with the local Hindus, the latest conquerors wanted to impose the religion of **Islam**. By AD 1225, the Delhi Sultanate had all of the Ganges River basin under its control.

In southern India, the Muslims never presented a real threat. Since the 8th century, Muslim Arab merchants had traded on the western Malabar coast. They were not interested in extending their influence beyond business, and when the Delhi Sultanate tried to extend its power south, it was repulsed.

The Delhi Sultanate lasted for 320 years and over six dynasties. The Mughal dynasty was the most successful. Today, around India and particularly Delhi, there is plenty of evidence of the cultural and artistic achievements of the Mughal empire.

The Mughal empire

The Mughal empire represented the high point of Islamic rule in India. There were six great Mughal rulers who oversaw a golden age of building, art and literature. At its height, under Emperor Akbar's reign (1556–1605; see box opposite), the Mughal empire expanded to an extent seen previously only under Asoka and later under the British. The Mughals' passion was building, and they constructed some of India's greatest buildings, including one of the world's most famous, the Taj Mahal (see page 99).

The founder of the Mughal empire was Babur. His reign lasted only three years, from 1527 to 1530, but he was responsible for defeating the sultan of Delhi. His grandson, Akbar, extended and consolidated the empire. Akbar was skilful in subduing the Rajputs of Rajasthan and then diplomatically made

The Mughal empire

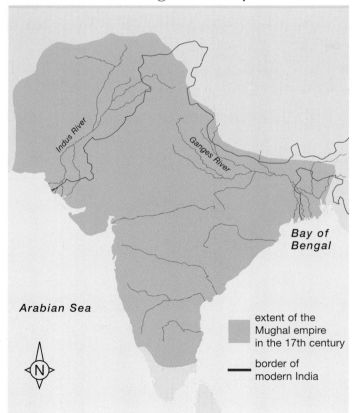

Indus River

Ganges River

Bay of Bengal

Arabian Sea

extent of the Mughal empire in the 17th century

border of modern India

N

Emperor Akbar

Akbar became emperor in 1556 when he was only thirteen. He ruled the Mughal empire until 1605. When he was only fifteen, Akbar conquered a large part of central India, and then went on to take control of the state of Rajasthan. In order to conquer the neighbouring state of Gujarat, Akbar marched 1000 km (600 miles) in nine days from his newly built capital, Fatehpur Sikri, with 3000 horsemen.

Akbar's skills were not restricted to his military prowess. He established an efficient system of government and was also a skilled diplomat. Akbar realized there were too many Hindus in India to ever convert them to Islam. Instead of treating them as second-class citizens, he married a Hindu woman and integrated the Hindus into his empire by using Hindu advisers and generals and employing Hindus as administrators. He spoke to leaders of other religions and established religious tolerance in the empire. Although he could not read or write, Akbar promoted the arts and literature. He encouraged the development of the Mughal school of miniature painting – a skill that was introduced from Persia (modern-day Iran) – and is the central figure in the miniature painting above.

the defeated Rajput generals into the governors of his newly conquered territories.

Akbar's son, Jehangir, took the throne after his father's death and followed his basically good and enlightened rule, although he spent little time outside the state of Kashmir. Shah Jahan, who reigned from 1627 to 1658, secured the throne by executing all his male relatives. A firm and successful administrator, and responsible for some of the marvels of Mughal architecture, Shah Jahan was eventually imprisoned by his second son, Aurangzeb, in the Agra Fort across the river from the Taj Mahal, which Shah Jahan had built. He spent his last seven years able to glimpse the distant Taj only as a reflection on a small piece of glass.

When Aurangzeb inherited the throne in 1658, the Mughal empire was becoming increasingly difficult to

A miniature of Shah Jahan ('Ruler of the Universe') and his beloved wife, Mumtaz Mahal, for whom he built the white marble mausoleum the Taj Mahal. She died giving birth to their fourteenth child.

rule. Intent on expanding the empire's boundaries still further, Aurangzeb imposed heavy taxes on his subjects to pay for his military campaigns. This, combined with his obsession to make India a Muslim state, led to the empire's downfall. Revolts and rebellions broke out across the empire and these were increasingly difficult to stop. After Aurangzeb's death in 1707, the Mughal empire's fortunes declined. Although there continued to be Mughal emperors, they had no effective power.

The Maratha empire

In the Maharashtra region of west India, non-Brahmin (non-priestly) castes organized themselves into a formidable fighting force under their legendary leader, Shivaji. In the 18th century, the Marathas moved quickly to subdue other areas. Such was their fighting prowess that other states were soon paying them 'protection money' to prevent their raids.

By 1751 the Marathas controlled enough of India that their territory could be called an empire. Sensing the weakness of the Mughals in the north, foreigners invaded the territory of the Mughals. When Afghan forces invaded Delhi in 1757, the Mughals employed the Marathas to defend their territory. In 1761 Afghan armies met the Marathas in battle. The complete defeat of the Marathas brought their imperial aspirations to an end. It was this power vacuum at the end of the 18th century that allowed the European powers who traded in India to enter the area.

The Maratha empire controlled much of central India but failed to halt the influence of the European powers on the subcontinent.

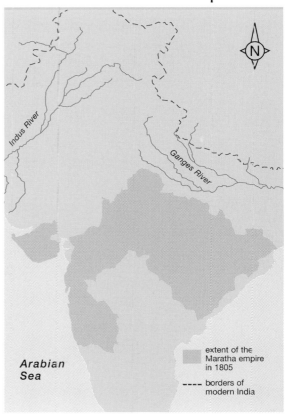

The Maratha empire

Indus River

Ganges River

Arabian Sea

N

extent of the Maratha empire in 1805

---- borders of modern India

THE EUROPEANS

In 1498, the Portuguese explorer Vasco da Gama (1460–1524) landed at Calicut, in the state of Kerala on the south-west coast of India. The Portuguese explorer reached Calicut by sailing around the southern tip of Africa, the Cape of Good Hope. The Portuguese were the first Europeans to set up permanent links with India. Early in the 16th century, they established a colony in the state of Goa, which they kept until 1961. They also established naval stations to the north. The Portuguese failed to make inroads into the rest of India, however, and it was other Europeans who established stronger trade links with India. European trade was very small compared to that of the Indian traders.

During the 17th century, the English, French, Dutch and Danish all set up East India companies to trade with India. They came to buy Indian textiles, dyes such as indigo and spices. Of the Europeans who came to India, only the British and French were serious contenders for power. The Dutch concentrated on the East Indies (present-day

The spice trade

Spices have been at the heart of Indian trade for thousands of years. India first became a trading partner with Western countries thanks to its wealth of spices. The fertile slopes of the Western Ghats produce black pepper, cardamom, cinnamon, cloves, garlic, turmeric and nutmeg. The earliest trade was with the Sumerians, Phoenicians, Arabs, Greeks and Romans. Traders from China, Portugal and England followed.

Explorers such as Marco Polo, Vasco da Gama and Christopher Columbus set sail from Europe in search of spices, which were highly prized in Europe as flavourings in cooking. In 16th-century Europe, spices were used to mask the flavour of rotting meat. The prices of most spices exceeded that of gold by weight. Traders were able to inflate prices because they controlled the supply.

In India spices are used both in cooking and in medicines. Indians believe that spices affect behaviour differently. They use spices when preparing food to produce the six tastes (*rasas*) of sweet, salty, bitter, astringent, sour and pungent, considered necessary to every meal.

Europeans in 17th-century India

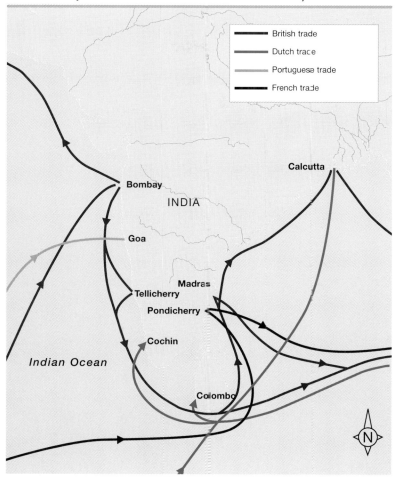

British trade
Dutch trace
Portuguese trade
French trade

Calcutta
Bombay
INDIA
Goa
Madras
Tellicherry
Pondicherry
Cochin
Indian Ocean
Colombo
N

While the French, Dutch and Portuguese controlled specific areas of the Indian coast, the British used military force to seize the Indian possessions of other European powers.

Indonesia), the Portuguese were content in Goa and Danish involvement was very small. As the Mughal empire broke into smaller states, the Mughal rulers could only look on as the Marathas, the French, the British and local governors fought for control of its former lands.

The British East India Company employed small armies to protect its commercial interests. The armies were often better equipped than their Indian counterparts, with the result that several Mughal rulers sought their protection. In return for stationing troops on their territory, the Mughal rulers paid money to the company, often at a very high price.

The British East India Company was established by 80 London merchants in 1599 and had 27 trading posts in India by 1647. By the late 17th century, the company had established a trading post at Fort William, which was later to become the city of Calcutta (Kolkata).

This late 18th-century Mughal painting shows an official of the East India Company riding on an elephant, surrounded by his Indian servants.

BRITISH RULE

The British presence in India began with trade, but once Britain became involved in the affairs of local Indian states to protect British trade, it began extending its territory. This process continued throughout the 18th century. Successive regional powers were brought under control of the British East India Company. Gradually, British interest in India stopped being purely commercial and started to encompass all aspects of Indian life. As this slowly happened, the British government started to assume more power from the East India Company.

The British defeated their main European rivals, the French, in a series of battles. In 1746, events in India brought France and Britain to war there. The French seized the British base at Madras (Chennai), but Britain regained it in 1749. A short peace followed before the Seven Years' War between the two powers on a worldwide basis from 1756 until 1763. The British emerged as victors following the Battle of Plassey in 1757, when they defeated the *nawab* (prince) of Bengal, who was responsible for the Black Hole of Calcutta (see page 38). At the time, Bengal was the richest of the Mughal provinces, and its wealth was being used by the British to finance their war against the French. In 1761, the British captured the east coast port of Pondicherry from the French, bringing the French challenge for control of India to an end.

Britain continued to expand its territory in India, but there was fierce opposition from Sikhs in the northern Punjab region, the Marathas in the west and the Mysore sultans of the south. The Marathas were not defeated until the 1816–18 war with the British. Their defeat owed more to internal divisions than to British military skill. By 1818, much of India was in ruins, and the British set about claiming it as their own.

Under British rule, India remained no more united than it had been previously. The British oversaw 562 princely states that were supposed to be independent but in reality came under strong British influence. The princely states remained in existence until independence in 1947 when, with the exception of Kashmir, they were included in the newly created countries of India and Pakistan.

In order to bring some unity to its huge colony and to maximize trade, the British set about building an infrastructure of railways and telegraph stations and improving roads and steamship services.

The princely states

On 1 November 1858, the first viceroy of India (the representative of the British king) announced the British government's new directive on India. Abandoning their previous policy of unification of India, the British now decided to support the local 'princes, chiefs and peoples of India', resolving not to intervene in religious matters. Christian missionaries were discouraged from working in the country for fear of Hindu and Islamic revolts. The British saw the rivalry of hundreds of local Indian states as 'natural breakwaters', preventing a united uprising against British economic domination. One condition of the statement was that the states and their princes must swear loyalty to the British Crown. The British built military bases around the country, living separately from most Indians. The local princes were free to settle local matters, while the British dominated trade.

They introduced British systems of policing, law and order and civil service. Indians were employed at low-ranking positions – they could not advance, for example, beyond a certain level in the army. On 7 March 1835, English was made the national language of India, thereby establishing British domination. Britain took over India's industries for its own profit. India's textile industry, for example, was destroyed by the compulsory **import** of British textiles. Resentment among Indians grew.

Divide and rule

The British realized that India was too important to be ruled by a private company. Henceforth, India was to be ruled by the British Crown, and in 1858, a representative, or viceroy, was sent to rule India on behalf of Queen Victoria. After the 1857 mutiny (see box below), the British used the lessons learned from the uprising to implement their divide-and-rule policy. The mutiny had

The 1857 mutiny

Less than 50 years after the British had ousted their European rivals from India, they suffered their first major setback – a large-scale uprising called the Indian Mutiny. The precise origins of the mutiny are uncertain, but one cause was distrust of the British. A rumour spread that the British were going to introduce new cartridges for the Indian sepoys' guns. Sepoys were Indians serving in the British Army. It was rumoured that the cartridges had to be waterproofed with a mixture of pig and cow fat, and the sepoys would have to bite the cartridge before loading. The cow is sacred to the Hindus, and the pig is unclean to the Muslims, so the action would have offended almost all Indians. In May 1857, 85 sepoys were thrown into jail in Meerhut, near Delhi, for refusing to use the new cartridges. The next day a mutiny started. During the following eighteen months, it spread through most of the army units across north India. Civilians joined in, but the mutiny failed because the Indians were not unified and many supported the British.

The 1857 mutiny was a key moment in India's history. It marked not only the end of the Mughal empire but also the end of the power of the British East India Company. The British government took overall control of India in 1858.

failed because of the lack of unity and trust between different groups of Indians. The British realized it would be to their advantage to keep different religious and racial groups at odds with each other. To this end, they denied Muslims opportunities for education and employment. This in turn created tension between Muslims and Hindus as the Muslims resented advantages bestowed on Hindus.

The days of the British Raj

The British empire in India had become the British empire of India. The British **Raj** – a **Hindi** word meaning 'rule' – began to turn India into a British colony in order to serve Britain's needs. In the early days of the British East India Company, male British colonists had sought to integrate themselves into the Indian way of life, whether it was by taking an Indian wife or by learning Hindi. As the British became more involved in India, new recruits from Britain made the five-month sea journey and

A colonial officer is waited on by Indian servants during the British Raj.

brought with them their wives and children. A separate society evolved. By and large, the British stopped mixing with the Indians and created in India a replica of British life thousands of kilometres away. They employed Indians as servants and socialized only with other Britons in their whites-only clubs.

The opening of the Suez Canal in 1869 cut the sea voyage from England to India from five months to five weeks, and more British expatriates arrived to work in the Indian Civil Service (ICS). Although the ICS was supposedly open to Indian recruits, the examinations were held in London, and only one Indian ever passed. Resentment among the Indian educated classes grew stronger.

Resistance to the Raj

In 1885, educated Indians from all over the country met in Mumbai (Bombay) to form the Indian National Congress Party. The idea for the party was born out of growing resentment towards the British. Ironically, this resentment had been aided by the common use of the English language. Indians from different parts of the country who had previously been unable to communicate with each other now used English to communicate. The newly formed party was made up largely of professional Hindus who wanted to gain more involvement in the civil service. The party split into a moderate element that wanted to work with the British, and a more radical, nationalist element that wanted to preserve all things Indian.

At the start of the 20th century, India's population fell as famine and plague killed many people. The British government failed to

The National Congress

The first Indian National Congress Party meeting had 73 representatives from every province of British India. Only two were Muslims, 54 were Hindus and the rest were Jains and Parsees. Delegates were wealthy, educated men – over half were lawyers. The Congress quickly became popular within India, despite the disdain of the British. By 1888, the number of delegates had risen to 1248. But not until the partition of Bengal in 1905 did the Congress achieve real concessions of power from the British.

South Asia in 1900

AFGHANISTAN

Kashmir

Punjab

TIBET

Baluchistan

United Provinces

NEPAL

BHUTAN

Sind

Bihar and Orissa

Rajputana

Bundelkhand

Bengal

Central Provinces

Burma

Bay of Bengal

SIAM

Indian Ocean

Bombay

Hyderabad

Goa

Madras

Mysore

Lower Burma

Travancore

Indian Ocean

Ceylon

N

provide any improvements in living conditions. When the viceroy, Lord Curzon, made Tibet part of the British empire in 1904, Indians began to realize that the British were more interested in expanding their territory than in the welfare of the Indian people.

In 1905, the British, continuing their divide-and-rule policy, decided to partition the state of Bengal and give most of the territory to the Muslims. Outraged, the Bengalis organized a boycott of British goods, particularly textiles. The Hindu boycott marked the beginning of the end of the Raj, although the Muslims largely supported the British. To this end, the Muslims, who, at this

India became a British Crown Colony after the mutiny of 1857. By 1900, former independent states such as Hyderabad and Rajputana had been absorbed into the British empire.

point, made up about a quarter of the population of India, founded their own political party, the All-India Muslim League, in 1906. They claimed to represent all Muslims, although many Muslims belonged to the Congress Party and challenged the claim of the league's name. The creation of two parties showed how successful the British divide-and-rule strategy had been.

The moves towards independence

The Liberal Party in Britain won the elections of 1906 with a large majority. The British government, now under Liberal Party control, ushered in some small reforms in India. At the same time, the British used severe repression to put down India's growing demands for self-rule. In 1911, worn down by continual opposition and violence, the British revoked the partition of Bengal. The move outraged Muslims, who had gained more power under the partition. When the British decided to move their capital from Calcutta (Kolkata) to Delhi the same year, Hindus were upset by the fall in property prices in the former capital.

Britain's promises to give India greater freedom were forgotten when the British went to war with Germany in 1914. Throughout World War One, Britain expected, and received, support from its Indian colony. About 1 million Indian soldiers fought for Britain. Indian troops suffered a disproportionately high casualty rate and experienced racism at the hands of their British officers. Despite this treatment, Indian soldiers were admitted to the ranks of British officers, beginning in 1917. The Indians fought willingly in the hope that Britain would grant them increased self-rule after the war in recognition of their sacrifice.

By 1918, a figure had emerged in India who was to transform the calls for self-rule into a fight for independence. Mahatma Gandhi (1869–1948) was to become the leader of the Congress Party and the architect of India's fight for independence (see box opposite).

India's contribution to the British war effort between 1914 and 1918 was immense. More than 1 million Indian troops were shipped overseas with 100,000 casualties and 36,000 fatalities. India also provided a huge amount of military supplies and revenue.

Mahatma Gandhi

Mohandas Karamchand Gandhi was born in 1869 in Gujarat into a wealthy and devout Hindu family. He studied and trained in London as a lawyer. In 1893, he gave up his very successful Mumbai law practice to travel to South Africa, where he spent the next 21 years campaigning for the rights of Indian workers, discriminated against because of their colour.

In 1914, he returned to India, where he was already famous for his non-violent protests in South Africa. Gandhi travelled across India to see for himself how people lived. He was appalled by the treatment of women and of the lowest caste of people, the Untouchables (see page 114), and fought for better treatment for both.

Known as 'Mahatma' (Great Soul), Gandhi adopted the dress of the Untouchables, a home-spun loincloth. By 1920, he had become a leading figure in the Indian National Congress. He promoted a policy of non-violence and non-collaboration with the British. The best example of this was the Salt March of 1930. Salt, a basic commodity, was a government monopoly on which the British imposed a tax. Gandhi marched 240 km (150 miles) to the coast, barefoot and dressed only in his loincloth, where he illegally gathered salt from the shore.

Imprisoned on numerous occasions, Gandhi also went on hunger strikes as a means of protesting. The British did not know how to manage his non-violence.

Through the 1930s, Gandhi became disillusioned with the Indian Congress and spent more time among the country's poor. With the outbreak of World War Two, Gandhi launched a 'Quit India' campaign against the British, but many of his supporters were imprisoned.

Gandhi himself was bitterly disappointed with the partition of India when it gained its independence in 1947 (see page 70). He felt the bloodshed as Muslims and Hindus fought was a sign of his failure. Gandhi was assassinated in 1948 by a fanatical Hindu supporter who objected to his religious tolerance of Muslims and other religions.

Unrest in India

In 1917, the British government announced that Indians were to have more say in the running of their country. The end of World War One, and US President Woodrow Wilson's assertion that every nation should have the right to determine its own affairs, led many Indians to think change was imminent. This belief was short-lived. Strikes in Mumbai's cotton mills in 1918 and 1919, inspired by new workers' rights created in Russia after the revolution of 1917, were put down. Worse was to follow.

On 13 April 1919, an illegal meeting was held by 20,000 unarmed men, women and children in Amritsar, the sacred capital of the Sikh religion in the Punjab. British troops, seeking revenge for the earlier killing of Britons in the city, opened fire on the meeting and continued to fire for ten minutes until their ammunition ran out. Almost 400 people were killed. At first the British failed to apologize for the massacre. This alienated more Indians, who joined the cause for independence.

The Golden Temple at Amritsar, spiritual centre of the Sikh faith, was built in the late 16th century. In 1919, the city of Amritsar became the scene of a bloody massacre of Sikhs by British troops.

The 1920s saw Indians continue to agitate for independence. Gandhi was imprisoned for civil disobedience in 1922, and on his release, spent much of the decade living in **ashrams** (secluded Hindu communities), where he developed a programme of hand spinning and weaving. This was intended to help revive India's textile industry and free it from the domination of Britain's own textile trade. Meanwhile, in Britain the economy was depressed following the end of the war, and many now questioned how long Britain could afford to keep its colonies.

Gandhi's Salt March of 1930 (see page 65) mobilized yet more support from millions of Indians. They resumed Gandhi's policy of non-violent non-cooperation. In 1935, the British passed an act of parliament that limited the amount of power Indians could have in official posts. In 1937 the Congress Party won a spectacular victory at elections in which some 30 million Indians were now eligible to vote. Realizing their position in India was becoming more vulnerable, the British organized meetings with Indian representatives to discuss independence. The election victory presented Gandhi's successor, Jawaharlal Nehru (1889–1964), now president of the Congress Party, with a dilemma as to whether to take up the seats in the Indian Congress (Parliament). To do so would appear to be supporting the British. Not to do so would mean losing the first chance to bring about change. When Nehru decided the Congress Party would participate in the Indian government, the move alienated many Muslims.

The architect of India's independence from Great Britain, Mahatma Gandhi (right) talks to his eventual successor, Jawaharlal Nehru, in Bombay in 1946.

Mohammed Ali Jinnah

Born in India in 1876, Mohammed Ali Jinnah became a successful lawyer in Bombay in the early years of the 20th century. He was a leading moderate in the Indian National Congress, mediating relations between Indians and the British. In 1913, Jinnah became leader of the Muslim League. The campaigns of Gandhi in the 1920s and 1930s alienated Jinnah, however, who eventually despaired of influencing the Hindu-dominated Congress. In 1940, Jinnah publicly adopted the idea of separating India into two nations, one Muslim (Pakistan) and one Hindu (India), as a goal, and in 1947 became governor-general of Pakistan.

The seeds of partition

In contrast, the Muslim League did badly in the Indian elections. Their leader, Mohammed Ali Jinnah (1876–1948), accused the government of Hindu bias. In 1940, the Muslim League announced its intention to create a separate independent state out of India's north-western and eastern territories, which were predominantly Muslim. The state was to be called Pakistan after the initials of the northern provinces – Punjab, Afghania, Kashmir, and Indus-Sind – and *stan*, the Persian word for 'country'. Tension and conflict between Hindus and Muslims was not new, but the idea of splitting India into two nations was.

Tension between the two groups was aggravated after the outbreak of World War Two in 1939. The Hindu Congress Party was angered by Britain's failure to consult it until after Britain had declared war on Germany, and it resigned its position in the government in protest at Britain's behaviour. Meanwhile, the Muslim League offered its support to the British. As the war went on, the British allowed the formation of local Muslim governments in the northern states in exchange for Muslim support. Jinnah would accept only total independence for the northern states.

When the war ended in 1945, Britain was no longer a superpower. Both the major world powers at this point, the USA and the former Soviet Union, supported India's demands for independence. In Britain the issue became pressing because the country could no longer afford to keep India.

Independence became inevitable. Gandhi was vehemently opposed to the division of India into Muslim and Hindu states, but Jinnah was intent on it.

In August 1946, a year after the end of the war, Jinnah launched 'Direct Action Day' – a series of peaceful rallies and demonstrations for a Muslim state. The day ended in violence with more than 4000 dead. Riots erupted in Calcutta (Kolkata) and Hindus massacred Muslims in Bihar and Uttar Pradesh. A bloody civil war spread throughout India as Muslims fought Hindus. Britain announced it would withdraw from India in June 1948, but the continuing violence led it to decide, in June 1947, that the **partition** of India into two separate countries was the only way to move. In 1947, Britain decided to withdraw, bringing India independence almost one year early.

The Calcutta police use tear gas during an attempt to set fire to a Hindu temple in August 1946. Over 200 were killed in the city's disturbances alone.

INDEPENDENT INDIA

India was declared independent on 15 August 1947. Pakistan had been granted independence the previous day. At independence, Muslims made up one-fifth of the total population of India, and although they formed the majority in parts of north-western and east India, many were scattered throughout the rest of the country. A straightforward split between a Muslim and Hindu region was impossible. Instead, Pakistan was given two regions – one to the west and one to the east (present-day Bangladesh) separated by 2000 kilometres (1200 miles) of Indian territory.

The Muslim states of East and West Pakistan were separated by 2000 kilometres (1200 miles) of Indian territory. East Pakistan seceded from West Pakistan in 1971, becoming the new nation of Bangladesh.

It is estimated that some 13 million people were then forced to migrate between India and Pakistan. Muslim, Hindu and Sikh openly fought each other, mainly in the partitioned states of Bengal and the Punjab. The bloodbath that followed left 1 million people dead and

Indian Partition 1947

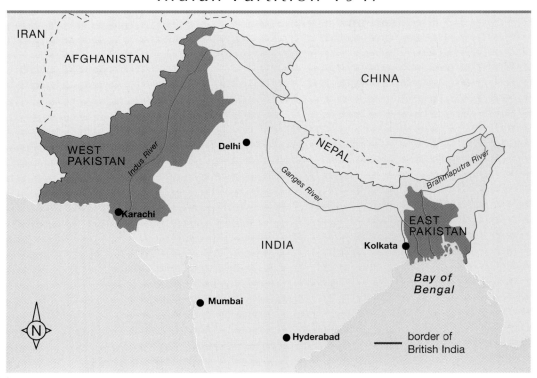

territorial claims unre-
solved. India and Pakistan
went to war almost imme-
diately over Kashmir (see
page 16). Gandhi walked
through the riot-torn
cities in an attempt to stop
the killing, but he was
assassinated by a Hindu
fanatic in January 1948.

Jawaharlal Nehru be-
came the first prime
minister of an indepen-
dent India. He succeeded
in putting in place a
centralized, government-
controlled economy. In
order to bring some
stability after the strife of
partition, he needed to
introduce a **constitution**

Muslims in India pile aboard any vehicle for Pakistan after the partitioning of India in 1947.

that would draw all the different strands of India
together and to build a strong economy. Nehru introduced three five-year plans to increase India's industrial
and agricultural output. Grain production increased
tremendously, and investment and foreign aid followed
in the early 1960s. Nehru accepted aid from both the
capitalist USA and the communist former Soviet Union.
India's north-eastern border was invaded by China in
1962 and it lost a small area of north-eastern territory.
In 1965, a dispute with Pakistan, which was supported by
the USA, pushed India closer to the former Soviet Union.

After Nehru's death in 1964, his daughter Indira
Gandhi (1917–1984; no relation to Mahatma Gandhi)
led the Congress Party to victory in 1966 and 1971. Her
socialist policies resulted in large annual increases in
industrial output and a Green Revolution fuelled by the
introduction of high-yield grain varieties (see page 79).

Indira Gandhi was the official hostess for her father, Jawaharlal Nehru, while he was prime minister (1947–1964), and took over his role two years after his death.

The formation of Bangladesh

In East Pakistan, the brutal repression of calls for independence from the dictatorship of General Yahya Kahn had by 1971 led to a flood of refugees from East Pakistan into India. In December 1971, Indian armed forces launched simultaneous attacks on East and West Pakistan and within two weeks had totally defeated the Pakistani army. This led to the formation of the new Muslim nation of Bangladesh in the former territory of East Pakistan.

Protests at rising inflation in India and corruption within Congress in the early 1970s led to the opposition's attempts to impeach Indira Gandhi. She declared a state of emergency in June 1975, suspending civil rights and introducing strict press censorship. The move lost her the 1977 elections in an atmosphere of protest, but the **coalition** led by Morarji Desai's Janata Party fell apart within two years, and by 1980, Indira was back in power. Four years later, she launched an ill-advised attack on Sikh protestors at the Golden Palace at Amritsar, who were demanding a separate Sikh state, Khalistan. The desecration of the Sikh's holy shrine led to the assassination of Indira Gandhi by her Sikh bodyguards in October 1984.

Indira was succeeded by her second son, Rajiv Gandhi (1944–1991), but increasing tensions at local levels and accusations of corruption led to the victory of V. P. Singh. His Janata Party, supported in coalition by the Hindu **fundamentalist** BJP party (see box opposite), lasted until late 1990. In the election campaign that followed in 1991, Rajiv Gandhi was assassinated by Sri Lankan extremists, angered by the Indian army's intervention in the Sri Lankan civil war.

Recent developments

The Congress Party swept back to power in 1991 under P. V. Narasimha Rao. He opened up the Indian economy to foreign investment, which provided a huge boost to industry. The 1990s also saw increased tension between Muslims and Hindus erupt into violence. Hindu fundamentalist parties such as the BJP and Shiv Sena gained increasing support as the situation escalated. Once again, there were charges of corruption against the Congress Party. These charges and the withdrawal of key agricultural subsidies led to a disaster for the Congress Party at the 1996 elections, with the BJP becoming the largest party in Congress for the first time. It attempted to form a coalition government with several smaller parties, but this administration received a vote of no confidence in 1997, leading to new elections in March of the following year.

Thirteen months later, Atal Behari Vajpayee's thirteen-party coalition was brought down by the Congress Party. This time the Congress Party was unable to form a

The BJP Party

The Bharatiya Janata Party, or BJP, is a Hindu nationalist party, meaning that it aims to favour the concerns of the Hindu majority instead of those of other religions. The party first won popularity in the late 1980s after allegations of corruption tainted the ruling Congress Party. The BJP gained additional notoriety internationally following its support of the destruction of a **mosque** in Ayodhya in 1992. Claiming that the Muslim temple had been constructed on the site of a previous Hindu temple, the BJP supported the destruction of the mosque and the building of a Hindu temple. The destruction of the temple prompted an outbreak of revenge attacks in Mumbai and Delhi in 1992, but many Hindus were impressed by the BJP and joined the party.

In May 1996, the BJP came to power briefly in a coalition, but this was short-lived. Again, in 1998, the BJP emerged as the largest party but without an overall majority. A further election was called for 1999, and the BJP leader Atal Behari Vajpayee became the new Indian prime minister of a multi-party coalition.

government, and elections followed for the third time in as many years. The elections produced a coalition of right-wing parties with Vajpayee remaining as prime minister.

POLITICS AND GOVERNMENT

Since its independence, India has been a federal **republic**. The country is split into 28 states and seven union territories. Indian national, or central, government is based on the British system. The federal government is led by the prime minister and a council of ministers, who are responsible to the two houses of parliament.

The People's Assembly (*Lok Sabha*), or lower house of the Indian Parliament, has 543 members who are directly elected by the Indian people and two members who are appointed by the president. They serve a five-year term. The Council of States (*Rajya Sabha*), or upper house, has no more than 250 members, of whom up to twelve are chosen by the president. The rest are directly elected. All members serve a five-year term.

The president serves a five-year term and is elected by the two houses of parliament and members of the regional parliaments through an electoral college. The president's duties are mainly ceremonial – he or she must follow the advice of the council of ministers and the prime minister.

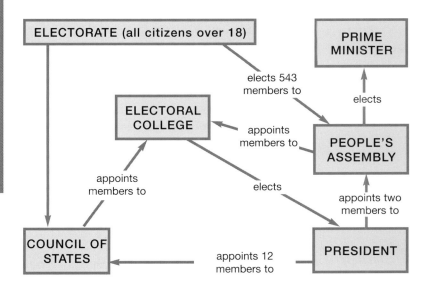

74

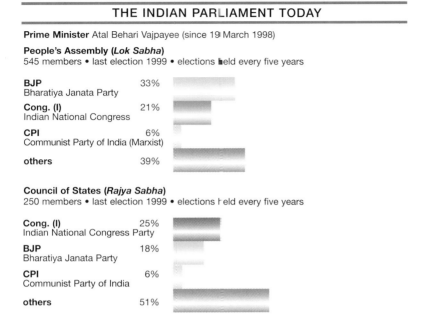

THE INDIAN PARLIAMENT TODAY

Prime Minister Atal Behari Vajpayee (since 19 March 1998)

People's Assembly (*Lok Sabha*)
545 members • last election 1999 • elections held every five years

BJP Bharatiya Janata Party	33%
Cong. (I) Indian National Congress	21%
CPI Communist Party of India (Marxist)	6%
others	39%

Council of States (*Rajya Sabha*)
250 members • last election 1999 • elections held every five years

Cong. (I) Indian National Congress Party	25%
BJP Bharatiya Janata Party	18%
CPI Communist Party of India	6%
others	51%

Indian politics is dominated by the BJP and the Congress Party. Both, however, rely on the support of smaller parties to form a government.

Each state has its own parliament. Some have two chambers like the national parliament. State governments are headed by a chief minister. If the affairs of a state are seen to be getting out of hand – as has happened in the state of Jammu and Kashmir – the federal government can intervene and impose direct rule from Delhi. Each state also has a governor appointed by the president.

Each state is responsible for health, education, forests and transportation excluding railways. The quality of services varies enormously – as can be seen in education. In Kerala literacy is 91 per cent, while in Bihar state it is only 62 per cent.

The main national political parties are: the BJP, Congress Party, Janata Dal Party, the Communist Party of India and the Bahujan Samaj Party, representing the caste of the Untouchables. In addition there are at least 37 state parties, and more than 300 other registered parties. Because of the high illiteracy levels in India, each political party uses a pictorial symbol. The BJP's symbol is a lotus flower, the Congress Party uses a hand and the Janata Dal Party has a wheel.

The Economy

'India has an immense reservoir of resources and inner strength. If we tap this reservoir, the benefit will be a hundred times more than we pay.'

Indian Prime Minister Atal Behari Vajpayee

At the end of the twentieth century, India's economy was the fifteenth largest in the world with a gross national product (GNP) of £223,000 million. A country's GNP is the value of all the goods and services that country produces in a year. Although India has the world's second-largest population, its GNP is relatively small. In comparison, China, the world's most populous country, has the seventh-largest GNP, and the USA, with the world's third-largest population, has the largest GNP.

The reason for India's relatively low GNP is that its economy is predominantly based on agriculture. All the world's leading economic powers are **industrial** nations. Industry is becoming increasingly important, and India is one of the world's top ten emerging industrial nations. Following changes to the way the economy was run in 1991, India opened up its economy to foreign investment. As a result, the economy grew for much of the 1990s.

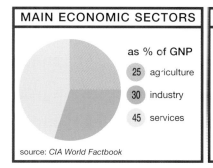

MAIN ECONOMIC SECTORS

as % of GNP

25	agriculture
30	industry
45	services

source: *CIA World Factbook*

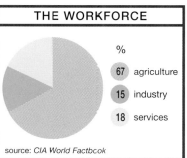

THE WORKFORCE

%

67	agriculture
15	industry
18	services

source: *CIA World Factbook*

India is the largest producer and consumer of tea in the world. The main growing areas are Assam, West Bengal, Kerala and Tamil Nadu.

INDIA'S ECONOMY AFTER INDEPENDENCE

After Indian independence, the first prime minister, Jawaharlal Nehru, created an economy planned and controlled by the national government. In the 1950s, Nehru tried to copy the former Soviet Union's planned industrial development using a series of 'five-year plans' to increase industrial production through more government control. He allowed private investment and control in agriculture and other 'non-essential' industrial sectors. Initially his plans were only partly successful. Three monsoons devastated Indian agriculture in the early 1950s, leading to the country's dependence on foreign aid for a few years. However, the economy picked up and a 'Green Revolution' in farming in the 1960s rapidly increased farm output, leading to surpluses in the 1980s.

India is the third-largest producer of cotton in the world after China and the USA. The crop forms the basis of the country's largest export, textiles.

Planning and foreign aid

The Indian government's role in the economy has traditionally been extensive. So vast is the country's population and so wide the range of economic enterprises in the country – from almost medieval agricultural practices to the most sophisticated hi-tech industries – that the government has played a major role in linking different areas of the economy and attempting to plan what will be produced in order to overcome the country's huge problem of poverty.

India was dependent on foreign aid for much of the late 20th century. Its diplomatic neutrality meant that aid was received from both the USA and the former Soviet Union. Initially this came in the form of food, but as India developed agriculturally, food was replaced by technological assistance and financial investment. Today India is still the third-largest recipient of international aid after China and Egypt, receiving over £937 million in 1997.

A deterrent to foreign involvement in the economy was India's high taxes on **imports**. These taxes added to the price of goods entering the country from abroad, limited foreign involvement in the economy and protected India's poor from the worst ravages of foreign exploitation. It also gave domestic industry the chance to develop without having to compete internationally with more efficient economies. However, in the long term, the Indian economy failed to keep up with international industrial developments, and its share of international trade declined sharply in the first 40 years of independence. The lack of foreign competition proved to have as many disadvantages as advantages.

MAIN TRADING PARTNERS

EXPORTS

%	
19.3	USA
6	United Kingdom
5.8	Hong Kong
5.6	Japan
63.3	others

IMPORTS

%	
9.5	USA
7.1	United Kingdom
6.8	Belgium
6.7	Germany
69.9	others

source: *Economist World in Figures*

India's main economic partners are the English-speaking nations of the UK and the USA.

The Green Revolution

For a huge agricultural nation such as India, the introduction in the 1950s and 1960s of new chemical fertilizers, the products of Western industry and high-yield seeds, developed by booming scientific research, was to have a revolutionary effect on rural areas. During the period of Indira Gandhi's premiership (1966–77), the government encouraged food production by paying farmers higher prices to switch to food crops. In addition,

EXPORTS (£ 000 million)	
● textiles	5.0
handicrafts	3.7
● gems and jewellery	3.2
● engineering goods	3.1
● chemicals	1.9
total (including others)	21.2

IMPORTS (£ 000 million)	
● machinery and equipment	5.7
crude oil and products	5.1
● gems	1.9
total (including others)	25.6

source: *Economist World in Figures*

Malnutrition,
a major cause
of ill health, is
widespread
among India's
poor. Conditions
in the shanty
towns are made
worse by a lack of
basic sanitation.

government-sponsored programmes taught farmers new scientific farming methods. While India used to import food in order to feed its people, the country is now self-sufficient in food. Food distribution among India's poor, however, is another matter. India's booming industrial economy has encouraged many peasant farmers to abandon rural poverty for the hopes of a better life in the city. Unfortunately, few succeed, and the vast **shanty** towns that surround India's larger cities are a testament to the country's enduring problem of feeding its people – now more a problem of dividing the available food rather than any overall shortage.

Dwellings in India's shanty towns, such as this site on Mumbai's coastline, are made of all manner of salvaged materials.

Industrial expansion

During the period of the Green Revolution, industrial output still lagged behind agriculture. Comments made by Nehru suggest that he did not believe industry to be so important in India's economy, and, as a result, it was largely left outside of the government's control. By the 1980s, although India continued with the five-year plans – in 1998 it was halfway through the ninth plan – economic reform and a relaxing of economic controls had started to take place. The process of opening up India to foreign investment and competition was started by the then-prime minister, Indira Gandhi, in the early 1980s and was continued by her successor, her son Rajiv Gandhi. However, by the end of the decade, those who had profited under the old inefficient system put the brakes on reform, and by the early 1990s, the economy was stricken by a fall in the value of the rupee and high price rises. The then-prime minister, Narasimha Rao, deregulated the economy in 1991. This meant decreasing government control, encouraging foreign investment, and cutting government spending. By the mid-1990s, the economy was booming and millions of people were benefiting from the changes. A whole new middle class was created who could afford cars and consumer goods that previously only the richest could afford.

Today, India has a wide range of industrial production ranging from textiles to rockets. The country has great expertise in computer technology, and Bangalore has become India's 'Silicon Valley' (see page 86). Millions of Indians living abroad contribute to the Indian economy as non-resident investors. However, alongside the booming Indian

The introduction of the free-market economy was strongly resisted by, among others, the Communist Party. It argued that it would destroy India's village-based communities.

Female office workers in Mumbai walk to work. Only 29 per cent of the Indian workforce is female, one of the lowest figures in the world.

stock market, the growing middle class and the visible levels of consumption, around half the population still lives in poverty, lacking many of the basics of life.

AGRICULTURE AND FISHING

Mahatma Gandhi said that the heart of India was in its villages. Although Indian cities are vast, sprawling places, with some of the highest population densities in the world, 75 per cent of all Indians still live in rural villages. The farmers in these villages practise subsistence farming – growing just enough crops for their own consumption. They depend on the monsoon for irrigation, and when it fails, the results are devastating not only for the villages but for the economy as a whole. Sixty-seven per cent of India's labour force of nearly 400 million work in agriculture, producing 30 per cent of GNP.

Crop varieties and fertilizers may have changed, but most Indian farming methods still follow age-old practices.

After 1947, large farms were broken down to enable more people to own small parcels of land to support themselves. Today, more than 80 per cent of India's farmland is held in units of fewer than 8 hectares (20 acres).

LAND USE

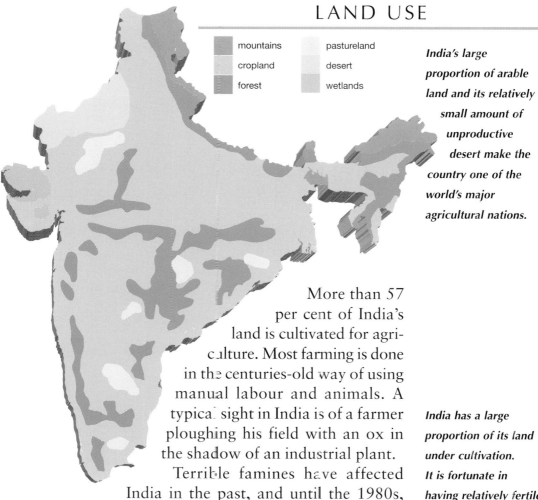

mountains
cropland
forest

pastureland
desert
wetlands

India's large proportion of arable land and its relatively small amount of unproductive desert make the country one of the world's major agricultural nations.

More than 57 per cent of India's land is cultivated for agriculture. Most farming is done in the centuries-old way of using manual labour and animals. A typical sight in India is of a farmer ploughing his field with an ox in the shadow of an industrial plant.

Terrible famines have affected India in the past, and until the 1980s, India had to import food grains. The innovative Green Revolution expanded irrigation of land and widened the use of fertilizer. This increased the production of food staples such as rice and wheat, and food production has doubled in the past twenty years. Since the 1980s, India has become a net exporter of rice and wheat. In addition, tea, coffee, cotton and sugarcane are grown and contribute to export earnings. Exotic fruits such as mangos, papayas, guavas and coconuts are grown for home use and for export.

India has a large proportion of its land under cultivation. It is fortunate in having relatively fertile soils thanks to flooding and silt deposits from rivers.

LAND USE

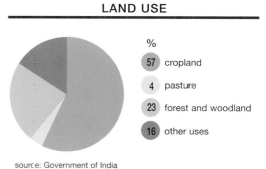

%
57 cropland
4 pasture
23 forest and woodland
16 other uses

source: Government of India

The fishing industry

India has thousands of kilometres of coastline, and in coastal areas such as Goa and Bengal, fresh fish and shellfish are widely eaten. India ranks among the top ten of the world's fishing nations with an annual catch of 3 million tonnes (2.9 million tons). Fish such as sardines, mackerel, bummalo fish – which is known as Bombay duck when dried – and shellfish such as lobster, prawns, crayfish and crab are common in Indian waters. In Bengal, fish are also reared on fish farms.

The Union Carbide factory in Bhopal was the site of a poison gas leak in December 1984 that claimed thousands of lives and injured tens of thousands of the city's inhabitants.

Manufacturing industry

Only 15 per cent of India's labour force work in **manufacturing** industries. Nevertheless, India produces a wide range of goods such as steel, vehicles, textiles and chemicals. Many foreign companies have factories in India because labour costs are much cheaper and health

MAJOR INDUSTRIES

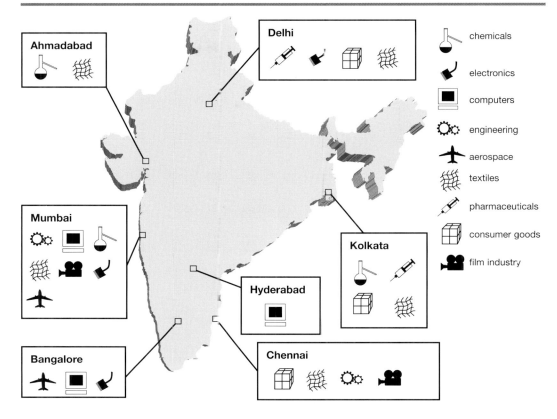

and safety regulations are not so strictly enforced. One result of this lax control was the disaster at the Union Carbide factory in Bhopal in 1984 (see opposite). More recently, campaigners have drawn attention to the use of child labour by Western corporations working in India.

Following economic reforms in the 1990s, industrial growth has been rapid. However, India has expanded from a small industrial base. One of the disadvantages of rapid industrialization is increased pollution. Delhi is now one of the most polluted cities in the world.

In addition to heavy industry, India excels in new technology, and many information technology (IT) companies, such as Microsoft, have Indian offices. The centre of the new technology is Bangalore (see page 86).

Another major industry is the film business (see page 101). More than 900 new films are made in India each

India's industry is still distributed around the old colonial centres. The production of textiles is a major industry in the villages.

Bangalore: India's Silicon Valley

Traditionally known as the garden city, Bangalore, the state capital of Karnataka, today is more often called India's 'Silicon Valley'. With a population of more than 5 million, it is one of the fastest-growing cities not only in India but also in Asia, attracting computer graduates from a wide area. The reason for its popularity among technology companies dates back to the 1960s, when the government made it the centre for key defence and telecommunications research. It grew into the science and technology centre of India.

Bangalore is currently home to some 200 IT companies. The largest software company, with a revenue in 1998 of £75.6 million, is the Indian-owned Infosys. The company's founders have set up a foundation to provide health and education for the poor. Many international companies use computer staff based in Bangalore because labour costs in India are cheaper. The staff are highly trained, and the time difference allows companies to operate for longer periods during the working day.

International IT companies employ highly educated graduates who enjoy Bangalore's cosmopolitan city life with its bars, nightclubs and shopping centres, which attract tourism and bring foreign revenue into the country. The downside to the city's expansion is an infrastructure that cannot cope. Water shortages, power cuts, poor roads and inadequate housing are everyday problems.

year, exceeding Hollywood's output. The biggest revenue earner is the 'Bollywood' film business based in Mumbai. South India has its own film industry, producing films in the main Dravidian languages of Kannada, Malayalam, Tamil and Telugu. There are 12,000 cinema theatres across India, and with millions of illiterate people among the population, visual entertainment is very popular. Indian films are one of the most popular forms of entertainment.

Mineral resources and energy

India is rich in many natural resources such as iron ore and bauxite. There are large deposits of coal that are expected to last for the next 100 years. Along with oil and gas deposits found off the Gujarat coast, hydro and nuclear power, firewood and even cow dung provide

ENERGY SOURCES

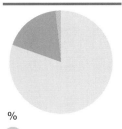

%

80 fossil fuels

18 hydro-electric power

2 nuclear power

source: *CIA World Factbook*

India's power. Where people do not have access to electricity, they use firewood, and the smell of burning wood at nightfall is common in cities and villages alike.

India is a major producer of gold, and everybody aspires to own gold, usually in the form of jewellery. Historically, India has been an important producer of gemstones. Gems and jewellery remain the country's third-largest export.

Communications and transportation

India's international airline is the government-owned Air India, which has daily flights to the rest of the world. To fly from London in England to India's capital, Delhi, takes approximately nine hours. The government-owned Indian Airlines is the largest domestic air carrier, and it competes with an ever-increasing number of private airlines to fly passengers across the country. Major airports are at Mumbai, Kolkata, Chennai and Delhi.

While flying is the fastest way of covering large distances across India, the most popular way to travel is by the government-operated Indian Railways, which carries 10 million passengers every day and is the fourth-largest railway company in the world. It is also the world's largest employer with more than 1.6 million

TRANSPORTATION

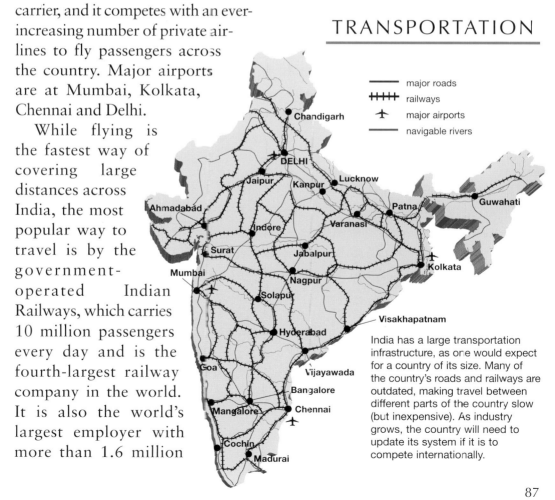

—— major roads
++++ railways
✈ major airports
—— navigable rivers

India has a large transportation infrastructure, as one would expect for a country of its size. Many of the country's roads and railways are outdated, making travel between different parts of the country slow (but inexpensive). As industry grows, the country will need to update its system if it is to compete internationally.

In India's remote areas, narrow-gauge railways (those with very closely spaced rails) are the norm. These provide a bumpier journey than the intercity express services.

employees. Indian trains are slow compared to the trains in Europe and other Western countries, but they are cheaper and offer a splendid way to see the country. Different-speed trains operate all over India, from the fast-link super-express Rajdhani Express, which runs between Delhi and Mumbai, to the very slow local trains. On long journeys, people turn the train into a temporary home – chatting, playing games, eating, drinking and sleeping to while away the hours. At each of the train's many stops, food sellers jump on the train to sell their home-made food. Subsidized fares means that travel is affordable for most Indians, although people sometimes travel on the train roof in order to avoid paying the fare.

Indian roads outside the major cities are often poorly maintained. Car ownership is low at only four cars per 1000 people (the UK has 697 per 1000 people), so the impact of private vehicles is slight. However, out of a total of 2 million kilometres (1.2 million miles) of main roads, only half is paved. All types of vehicles compete for space on the roads, and on remote routes it is not unusual to see a lorry or bus overtaking an elephant. Drivers have to swerve to avoid hitting cows walking along or even sitting on the road. In the cities, as more and more people own cars, it is often much quicker to walk than drive. Many people travel by buses, which operate all across India. Buses are a cheap but rundown and often very crowded means of transportation.

Tourism

India has always attracted visitors to see its varied landscapes and historical treasures, although not as many as might be thought. In 1998, there were only 2.3 million tourist arrivals, compared with France's 70 million. In addition, India attracts backpacking tourists rather than the luxury end of the tourist market. Indian politicians have realized that tourism generates income and creates jobs, so they raised the budget for India's Tourism Department by £9.4 million to £25 million for the 1999/2000 financial year. While the Taj Mahal (see page 99) is the top tourist attraction for visitors to India, the Indian Tourist Department wants to promote India's fifteen other World Heritage Sites, in addition to the countless monuments and lesser-known parts of the country. It is eager to improve road, rail and air links to key tourist sites.

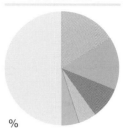

MAIN TOURIST ARRIVALS

%

16	United Kingdom
15	Bangladesh
9	United States
5	Sri Lanka
5	Germany
50	other

source: Government of India

An elephant ride is a must on any tourist's trip to India.

Arts and living

*'If there is a paradise on the face of the Earth.
It is this, oh it is this, oh it is this.'*

Inscription on the Red Fort, Delhi

India's ancient and great civilization has a rich cultural tradition that has been shared with the whole world. English, an Indo-European language, owes its origin to the ancient **Sanskrit** language of India, devised by the Aryans. The *Mahabharata*, which is one of India's oldest texts, was the first book known to be written in Sanskrit.

Modern Indian literature is just as likely to be written in English, a legacy of the British, as in any one of India's many languages. Indian-born writers such as Salman Rushdie (born 1947), Vikram Seth (born 1952) and R. K. Narayan (born 1906) are world renowned. At the other end of the spectrum, India's film industry is not only the world's largest but also constantly changing to meet the demands of its vast audiences.

The quality of daily life in India depends on how much money a person earns. Nevertheless, for those with money, food is plentiful and cheap, and there is a wide variation between regional dishes. Roadside food sellers are a common sight in the cities. Primary-school education is free and compulsory, but secondary school and universities charge fees, which means that often only the children of middle-class and rich families can afford them. The growth of the **IT** industry in Bangalore has attracted highly educated graduates from all over India, who previously would have had to emigrate to Europe or the USA to further their careers.

One of the chief means of preserving the caste system is the 'arranged marriage', where families choose a bride or groom for their son or daughter.

FACT FILE

- India's culture is one of the oldest in the world.

- The *Mahabharata* is one of the world's oldest stories.

- Cricket is India's most popular sport. The sport was introduced during the colonial period.

- The ancient Indian language of Sanskrit is one of the world's oldest languages.

- India's film industry is the largest in the world.

- Indians living in other parts of the world and wishing to find a partner from a similar social position will often place advertisements in India hoping to find a suitable partner.

The paintings in the Ajanta caves in northern Maharashtra state are masterpieces of Buddhist art. They date from around 200 BC to AD 650.

THE ARTS

India has a long artistic tradition that dates back thousands of years, and sophisticated examples of painting and sculpture can be found all over the country. The most distinctive buildings in India were built during the time of the Mughal emperors, which was a high point in Indian architecture. The British brought with them their own building styles, and many examples of Victorian buildings can be found in India's cities. Dance and music are an important part of life in India, and every region has its own songs and dances.

Literature

Ancient Sanskrit was the first-known language of India. Its literature influenced all of ancient India's political, religious and social life. Before a written language developed, Sanskrit poems and hymns were memorized and recited. Historians are still unable to date accurately the earliest Sanskrit hymns. The most influential Sanskrit scripts, the *Vedas* (see page 46), deal with politics, economics, religion and medicine and probably reached their final form only around the 6th century BC – although they originated much earlier. They are still read today. For example, a type of medicine called **ayurvedic** (see page 105) – which is still practised in India today and is increasingly popular in **the West** – is discussed in the *Vedas*. When the *Vedas* were written down in Sanskrit, they became the first compositions in an Indo-European language.

The *Upanishads* date from between the 7th and 5th centuries BC. They contain the two great classics of Sanskrit literature, the epic Indian poems the *Mahabharata* and the *Ramayana* (see box page 94). The latter was written by the poet Valmiki, who had a deep influence on the religious and cultural life of India. Both epic poems continue to be Hindu Indians' most loved stories.

The *Mahabharata*, a poem of more than 220,000 lines, recounts the battle between the forces of good and evil represented by the Pancavas, who are the heroes, and the Kauravas, the devils. When the *Mahabharata* was made into a television series that ran for many weeks, all of India came to a standstill as illiterate villagers and sophisticated Delhi residents alike were glued to the television set. The *Bhagavad Gita* – the Hindu holy book – is an episode from the *Mahabharata*.

These boys from Imphal in Manipur state in north-eastern India are portraying the Pandava brothers from the Indian epic the Mahabharata. *The brothers eventually triumph over their adversaries, the evil Kauravas.*

The *Ramayana*

The *Ramayana* tells the story of good versus evil in an epic poem that is widely seen to be South Asia's first literary poem. It tells how the god Rama was banished from his father's kingdom and leaves the city with his wife, Sita, and his helper, Hanuman, the monkey god (Hanuman crouches next to Sita in the illustration shown here). The evil Sri Lankan King Ravana kidnapped Sita. Supported by an army of monkeys led by Hanuman, Rama defeated Ravana and rescued Sita. Rama emerged from the victory as the embodiment of the perfect man (*Parushottama*). He is a perfect son, brother and king, and the poem concentrates on his kindness and compassion. Like the *Mahabharata*, the *Ramayana* was made into a television series that attracted a huge audience who loved the dramatic battle between good and evil.

Until the 18th century, Persian was the language of the princely courts in India, and classical Persian literature was the dominant influence. Although he could not read or write, the emperor Akbar (see page 53) was the greatest champion of literature of all the Mughal emperors. During the colonial period, English became the dominant language of the rich and well educated. As the use of English spread, Indians who previously had not been able to understand each other's language were able to communicate. Today, this use of English has helped many Indian writers reach an international audience and discuss ideas with one another in a common language.

India has many internationally renowned writers whose work is read far beyond India. One of the most popular is R. K. Narayan, who set his novels and short stories in the imaginary south Indian town of Malgudi. Malgudi is full of eccentric characters, and Narayan, writing in English, entertains the reader with details of the town's daily life. Modern writers such as Salman Rushdie, Vikram Seth and Arundhati Roy (born 1961) are better known in Europe than in India. They, too, write in English. Indian writers are engaged in a heated debate. Some think Indian literature should be written in one of India's native languages, while others believe English is the best language to use because it alerts the English-speaking world to the quality of India's writers.

Rabindranath Tagore

Despite being educated in England, Rabindranath Tagore (1861–1941) wrote in his native Bengali language. Tagore was the author of numerous novels, essays, plays and of India's national anthem, but he considered himself a poet. In 1913 he was the first Indian writer to win the Nobel Prize for Literature. Prime Minister Nehru, also a published author, wrote of Tagore: 'Tagore and Gandhi have undoubtedly been the two outstanding and dominating figures in the first half of the 20th century ... [Tagore's] influence over the mind of India, and especially of successive rising generations, has been tremendous. Not Bengali only, the language in which he himself wrote, but all the modern languages of India have been moulded partly by his writings.'

This is Tagore's poem 'The Kiss' (from *Kadi O Komal,* 1886).

Lips' language to lips' ears.
Two drinking each other's heart,
    it seems.
Two roving loves who have left home,
    pilgrims to the confluence of lips.
Two waves rise by the law of love to
    break and die on two sets of lips.
Two wild desires craving each other
    meet at last at the body's limits.
Love's writing a song in dainty letters,
    layers of kiss-calligraphy on lips.
Plucking flowers from two sets of lips
    perhaps to thread them into a chain
    later.
This sweet union of lips is the red
    marriage bed of a pair of smiles.

Art and architecture

India's ancient art and architecture were created for a religious purpose. The Buddhists, Hindus and **Muslims** all created their own art. The first stone monuments were built in Emperor Asoka's reign in the 3rd century BC, and decorated pillars such as the Asokan pillar at Sarnath survive today. Little of the Buddhist art that flourished throughout India survives, and much of the early Hindu architecture was destroyed by the invading Muslim armies.

India's painting, sculpture and architecture are unique because they show a consistency of style over thousands of years. Surviving ancient cave paintings and sculptures have much in common with more recent art. The historian D. D. Kosambi made the point: 'For no other country is the peculiar survival and expansion of prehistory ... so clearly discernible [noticeable]. This is the special historical and social character of India.'

The **murals**, or wall paintings, and sculptures in the caves at Ajanta and Ellora, in west India, are the finest examples of ancient Indian art. The Ajanta murals date from as early as 300 BC. They tell the story of the Buddha's

India's humid climate has had a profound influence upon its architecture. Few early buildings survive because so many of them were made of wood.

The Kailash Temple is Ellora's masterpiece. Started in the 8th century AD, it was hewn from a single block of stone and took over 100 years to complete.

life and the life and culture of the people of the time. The later Ellora caves are outstanding sculptures that were hewn out of a long cliff that stretches over a distance of some 3 kilometres (1.8 miles). Carved more than 1000 years ago, they depict Hindu and Buddhist religious themes. These delicate stone carvings took centuries to complete. In one cave, the Kailash Temple was carved from a single vast piece of rock. It took 7000 stone cutters more than 100 years to complete the Kailash Temple (see opposite).

Indian pottery

The art of pottery is connected both with India's most ancient myths and with the daily life of modern Indians. Brahma, the creator in the Hindu religion, is often called *prajapati*, the potter, and is believed to have made the first man and woman from clay, who then gave birth to a line of potters. In India today, terracotta is still largely used for containers as it keeps liquids cool. Potters also create small figurines that are used in places of worship, and potters may even intercede between the gods and the worshipper. At the harvest festival of Pongal, it is customary to smash all the pots in the household and replace them with new ones.

Sophisticated sculpture is found throughout India. In Khajuraho, in east India, is a group of Hindu temples built over 100 years between AD 950 and 1050 during the Chandela dynasty (see page 50). Famous for their erotic carvings, the temples are magnificent examples of intricate stonework that depict life in all its richness 1000 years ago. In Mahabalipuram, on the coast south of Chennai, is a huge stone frieze, or wall decoration, that dates from the 5th century AD. Called *Bhagiratha's Penance*, or *Descent of the Ganges*, the detailed carved frieze measures some 29 metres (95 feet) long and almost 7 metres (23 feet) high.

Little survives of India's ancient architecture. Some Hindu religious buildings, dating from the 6th century BC, are still standing in south and east India. The most distinctive architecture to have survived into the modern day belongs to the much later Mughal empire. When the Muslims invaded, they destroyed most of the temples and stripped jewels from buildings. Muslims built their mosques out of the temple stone and used the jewels for their own buildings. The great period of Islamic architecture in India fused Islamic design with traditional Indian designs. Mughal emperors used local craftsmen and builders to carry out their designs. The pinnacle of this fusion was the Taj Mahal (see opposite).

European influence

The Europeans in India showed little interest in mixing European architectural traditions with Indian ones. The Portuguese built several churches in Goa that look as though they have been transplanted from Portugal to India. The British left their mark on India's cities. Mumbai (Bombay), Kolkata (Calcutta) and Chennai (Madras) all have examples of British Victorian architecture in railway stations, churches and administrative buildings that made no concession to their being in India. Mumbai even had its own double-decker red buses, which are still in use today, modelled on the London buses.

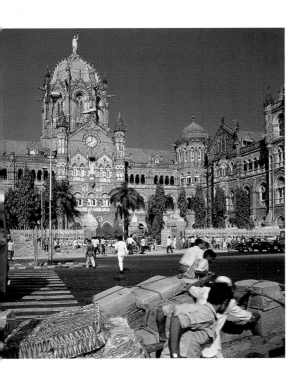

The Chatrapathi Shivaji Terminus (or Victoria Terminal) in Mumbai was built by the British in 1887. It is a bizarre medley of the European styles that were popular in Victorian Britain.

When the British moved their capital from Kolkata to New Delhi in 1911, they built the new capital to reflect their domination over India. It was designed by British architects Edwin Lutyens and Herbert Baker from 1921 to 1929. They did not want to include any Indian architectural details. Opposition, however, forced the British architects to compromise and include some Indian details, although these were largely superficial additions to the classical buildings.

After India's independence, Indian architects tried to break away from colonial influence but were unsure of the direction they wanted their new buildings to take. The government commissioned foreign architects to design new buildings, such as the Swiss-born Le Corbusier (1887–1965), who designed the city of Chandigarh.

The Taj Mahal

Recognized around the world as the ultimate symbol of love, the Taj Mahal is actually a tomb. It was built by the Mughal Emperor Shah Jahan to commemorate his wife, Mumtaz Mahal, who died in childbirth (see page 54).

The Taj Mahal marks the high point of Mughal architecture. Started in 1631, the tomb was built in white marble that was carried by 1000 elephants from Rajasthan some 300 km (180 miles) away. Intricate floral patterns made out of precious stones from all over the world decorate the marble. Twenty thousand workers took seventeen years to construct the mausoleum, which was not completed until 1648.

According to legend, Shah Jahan planned to build a black marble tomb for himself. He never did. His tomb lies beside that of his wife inside the Taj Mahal, where it is visited by millions of tourists each year. Today, conservationists are worried about the future of the Taj because increased pollution from nearby factories and vehicle emissions are destroying the marble. Strict rules are now in force for local industries, and polluting vehicles are not allowed within 1.6 km (1 mile) of the building.

Ravi Shankar

Born in Varanasi in 1920, the classical sitar player Ravi Shankar was described by the Beatles' George Harrison as the 'godfather of world music'. Shankar first came to prominence in the early 1960s through his collaborations with the violinist Yehudi Menuhin. His influence was heard on the Beatles' 1965 song 'Norwegian Wood'. But his own work reached a worldwide audience with performances at the Monterey Pop Festival in 1967, at Woodstock in 1969 and at the Concert for Bangladesh in 1971. Shankar has written for opera, dance and film. He has won two Emmys, and is an honorary member of the American Academy of Arts.

Indian music always has a constant drone sound, which is a reference for the audience and among the players. It is often played on a *surmandal*, an instrument like a zither.

Dance and music

Many Indian occasions call for dance and music: weddings, births, religious processions, harvest time, welcoming a guest and going to a new house are just some of the events that are celebrated with two of India's oldest art forms. Indians believe that sincere practice of the arts leads to the highest spiritual experience. Indian music and dance reflect the joy of life. Each Indian village has its own music and dances.

Indian dance varies from region to region. Classical Indian dance is generally divided into two types: *tandav*, which is associated with strength and masculinity, and *lasya*, which is more delicate and considered more feminine. There are four main schools of classical dance, *Bharata Natyam*, which is *lasya*; *Kathak*, which combines Muslim and Hindu influences and is both *lasya* and *tandav*; *Kathakali*, which originated in the 17th century, is usually based on stories from the epics and is danced by men; *Kuchipudi* is a dance also created in the 17th century and generally danced by men. In addition to the classical dances, there is a huge range of folk dances performed at local level, many of them based on local stories and traditions.

Indian music is deeply religious. The **sitar** was invented in the 13th century. It is a stringed instrument and has six or seven main strings, four of which are played for melody, while the other two or three provide a drone or rhythm. Other instruments include the *subahar*, a type of bass sitar, the *sarod*, which is smaller, and an oboe-like instrument called the *shehnai*. The **tabla** is a set of two small drums, played with the hands. Musical performances are often intimate affairs with the audience sitting on the floor close to the musician.

The film industry

The main centre of Indian filmmaking is Mumbai, home of the *masala* film, which is also known as Bollywood. *Masala* means 'mix', and a masala film contains a little bit of everything – romance, action, singing and dancing. This type of film is a 'feel-good' film: the bad guy always gets found out, and the good guy always gets his girl. The films are usually at least two hours long because, besides the main plot, there are always sub-plots that all have to be resolved by the end.

Only 5 per cent of films made are big box-office hits. To maximize the chances of a hit, film directors use India's most famous film stars whenever they can. This means that popular actors may work on many different films at the same time. One of India's most popular actors, Shashi Kapoor, was once signed up for 140 films at one time.

The film industry based in Chennai (below) – with 36 permanent sets, Asia's largest – caters to the southern Indian languages, while films made in Mumbai are in Hindi.

One former actress, Jayalalitha Jayaram, capitalized on her popularity by going into politics in the state of Tamil Nadu, where she was briefly chief minister.

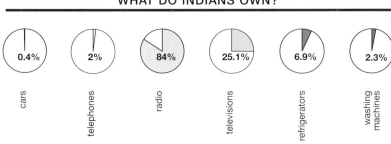

WHAT DO INDIANS OWN?

0.4% cars — 2% telephones — 84% radio — 25.1% televisions — 6.9% refrigerators — 2.3% washing machines

source: *Encyclopedia Britannica*

Basic nutrition remains the priority for the vast majority of Indians.

HOW INDIANS
SPEND THEIR
MONEY

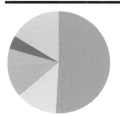

%
- 50.9 food and drink
- 13 transportation
- 9.8 housing
- 5.7 clothing
- 4.2 health
- 16.4 recreation/culture

source: *Encyclopedia Britannica*

Another film industry exists in India that is very different from those in Chennai and Mumbai. Disillusioned with the commercialism of the *masala* films, a break-away group of filmmakers created India's New Wave cinema, determined to show the reality of India. The most famous director of the New Wave was Satyajit Ray (1921–92), who was awarded an honorary Academy Award just before he died. Films such as *Pather Panchali* (*The Song of the Road*) brought not only Ray but also India to the attention of the world's film-goers.

The media

In a country in which almost half the population is illiterate, television plays a very important role in the media. Even the poorest village has at least one television set. The national channel, Doordarshan, broadcasts in both national and regional languages. Television has become increasingly popular since the introduction of satellite television in the 1980s. Satellite television has opened up the Western world to Indians, and many Indians prefer to watch Star TV, CNN or the BBC, instead of Doordarshan.

Newspapers and magazines, written in English and India's national and regional languages, are very popular. The best-known daily English-language newspapers are the *Times of India* and the *Indian Express*. English-language magazines such as *India Today* are also widely read.

EVERYDAY LIFE

Daily life in India depends on how much money a person has. For the poorest third of the nation, each day is a struggle to feed the family. The poor live from day to day because they do not have enough money to plan for the future. At the other end of the spectrum, the rich live extremely comfortable lives, looked after by many servants. In between is the growing middle class, which increasingly looks to Europe and the USA for its role models.

Sports and leisure

There is one sport that dominates India's sporting calendar – cricket, which was once described as 'polite baseball'. Brought to India by the British, cricket is a national obsession, especially in Mumbai. Whenever the Indian team is playing, crowds will gather around any shop that has a television, and people carry little radios so they can keep up to date with the latest score.

In every village and city, boys play cricket on any piece of empty land, using whatever they can as equipment. Many dream of being a top professional player.

Kabadi

Kabadi is a version of playing tag and is the most played game in India. Its popularity stems from the fact that it does not require any equipment, there are very few rules and anybody can play. Two teams of any number can play, though seven is the norm. Each team stands on either side of a central line. One person crosses to the other team's side and the object of the game is to stop him or her from getting back to their own half of the field. The opposing team chases the person, and if it catches and 'tags' them, they are out of the game. The team with the most players left wins.

India has one of the world's best cricket teams and won the World Cup, which is held every four years, in 1983. Matches against Pakistan are the most keenly fought with an intense rivalry between the two teams. India has produced some world-class international cricketers, including Sunil 'Sunny' Gavaskar (born 1949), Kapil Dev (born 1959) – who led the Indian team to victory in the World Cup in 1983 and was named the Wisden Indian player of the century in 2002 – and Sachin Tendulkar (born 1973).

Other games played in India include football, hockey – India's men's hockey team has won the Olympic gold medal eight times – tennis and polo, which is played on horseback.

Health and welfare

In India, health and welfare depend on two things – where a person lives and how much money he or she earns. Rich city dwellers enjoy the best medical treatment, while for poor villagers, the nearest doctor may be many kilometres away.

Each Indian state is responsible for its own health care, and is headed by a surgeon general. People usually have to pay for health care in India, but there is some provision for free medical care. Most small towns have a government-run hospital that can treat common diseases such as diarrhoea and malaria. There are also some charitable hospitals in the big cities that charge fees according to how much a person earns. A person's income determines the class of hospital bed he or she gets. In cities, doctors operate private clinics, and every consultation must be paid for. Private medical insurance does not exist across India, although it is starting to appear in the larger cities. In Mumbai, for example, many private companies take out medical insurance policies for their employees.

In India at the beginning of the 21st century, many people still die from hygiene-related illnesses, such as typhoid. In an effort to prevent this, health workers now visit remote villages to teach local people the importance of clean water, sewerage and drainage. Health workers also try to educate villagers about birth control.

Life expectancy in India varies according to how much a person earns. In 2001, men were expected to live to 62.2 years and women to 63.5 years. Women have an average of 3.04 children, and India's population continues to grow at about 17 million people a year.

The reasons for this growing population are many, but one primary cause is the high infant mortality rate at 63 deaths per 1000 children born (compared with 6 in the United Kingdom). This encourages those Indians who live in poverty to have many children in order to ensure that they have enough family members to farm the land and also to care for their parents in old age.

Ayurvedic medicine

The ancient *Vedas* (see page 46) contain numerous references to disorders and their treatment. Ayurvedic medicine, which is based on the teachings of the *Vedas*, is an entire medical system. It aims to prevent disease by maintaining in the body the balance of the five elements of space, air, fire, water and earth. This is done through a variety of practices, including meditation, yoga, herbal remedies and diet. The five elements are grouped into three *doshas* – *vata* (space and air), *pitta* (fire and water) and *kapha* (water and earth) – fundamental biological energies that regulate an individual's life processes. Historically, ayurvedism was important because it marked the movement of Indian medicine away from medical practice based on superstition and towards medicine based on physical observation of the individual's symptoms. During the period AD 100 to 500, Indian medicine was far more advanced than that in the West. There existed a detailed knowledge of human anatomy and surgical techniques, with simple operations to remove kidney stones or cataracts being performed.

Education

Primary-school education in India is compulsory. There are currently 573,000 primary schools out of a total of 820,000 schools. Primary-school education is free. In the countryside, lessons are sometimes taught under the shade of a tree because a schoolhouse is too expensive to build.

Secondary-school education is not free. Parents must pay for schoolbooks and tuition. Most schools insist that pupils wear a school uniform, which must also be paid for. Secondary-school education is not compulsory, although the government is attempting to make it so. At present, the quality of education secondary-school pupils receive depends on the state. In Kerala state, for example, which has a **communist** state government, a high premium is placed on education and almost all Keralans (91 per cent) are literate (can read and write). In contrast, in Rajasthan in the north-west, the literacy rate is only 62 per cent.

Teachers are well respected in India. People look up to the guru (teacher) because of his or her knowledge. Many children are very eager to learn because education offers a way to improve their job prospects.

Adult literacy

The lack of education of many Indians is an ongoing problem for the Indian government. It has launched literacy campaigns to teach people to read and write, but with limited success. Operation Blackboard was launched in 1987 to bring literacy to 100 million adults aged between 15 and 35. Ten years later, it had failed because of lack of money. India's literacy rate now stands at 52%, although among women this falls to 37.7%.

Child labour

Often a poor family's immediate need to feed itself every day means that all the children must go out to work instead of going to school. Even if illiterate parents understand the benefit in extra salaries an education could bring their children, they need income today. They send the children onto the streets to sell gum, trinkets or polish shoes – anything that might earn a few rupees.

In 1986, the government acted to make it illegal to employ children under the age of fourteen in hazardous industries. Nevertheless, hundreds of thousands of poor and uneducated children continue to work in India today. For example, it is estimated that the carpet-weaving industry illegally employs 300,000 children. Children are employed because their small hands are able to weave the intricate patterns. They work very long days in bad conditions with poor light, few breaks and for very little money.

There is also a problem in that Western companies working in India have been less than scrupulous about checking the real age of employees in their factories, arguing that this is the responsibility of local government. This is particularly the case in the textile and garment industries producing goods for the Western markets.

University education is not free, and usually only middle-class or rich students can afford to go. The standard of further education is very high in India, and many students go on to postgraduate work both in India and overseas. Medicine, law and information technology (IT) are the most popular subjects for students. Many medical students leave India for successful careers as doctors and surgeons in Europe and the USA. Similarly, many computer graduates emigrated to California's Silicon Valley to further their careers, although now many are returning to Bangalore's Silicon Valley to help boost India's highly successful IT business (see page 86).

Despite the low proportion of Indians attending university, higher education has expanded tremendously since independence in 1947. The number of universities has increased sevenfold. There are rigorous tests for entry to university, but the number of students enrolling has increased by fifteen times.

EDUCATIONAL ATTENDANCE

Further (university) 7%

Secondary school 49%

Primary school 100%

How to say ...

Here are a few words of Hindi, India's national language, using the English alphabet. The words would normally be written in a different script, so the suggested pronunciation here is only approximate.

Hello/goodbye *Namaste*

How are you? *Aap kaiseh hein?*

OK *Acha*

Yes *Han*

No *Nahin*

Please *Mehabarni seh*

Thank you *Dhanyavaad/shukriyaa*

Don't worry *Koi baat nahin*

Sorry *Kshamaa kijiyeh*

You're welcome *Aaap ka swagat hai*

Do you speak English? *Kya aap Angreji bolte hai?*

I don't understand *Meri Samajh men nahin aaya*

What is your name? *Aapka shubh naam kya hai?*

My name is *Meraa naam...hai*

One *Ek*

Two *Do*

Three *Tin*

Four *Char*

Five *Panch*

Six *Chhe*

Seven *Saat*

Eight *Aath*

Nine *Nau*

Ten *Das*

Sunday *Ravivaar*

Monday *Somvaar*

Tuesday *Mangalvaar*

Wednesday *Budhvaar*

Thursday *Guruvaar*

Friday *Sukhravaar*

Saturday *Shanivaar*

National holidays and festivals

India has very few officially recognized national holidays, but it does have hundreds of different festivals, celebrated at various times across the country. Some of India's festivals are linked to the changing seasons, such as *Vasant Panchami* in February, when people mark the arrival of spring (*Vasant*) by wearing yellow clothes. Others celebrate religious dates such as the *Buddha Jayanti*, the first night of the full moon in either April or May that marks the birth of Buddha. *Diwali*, the Hindu festival of lights, is celebrated in October or November, particularly in north India, and is the happiest of Indian festivals. Indians believe it is important to celebrate the festival properly to encourage the gods to return to Earth. Rows of lamps or candles are lit in remembrance, and *rangoli*s (chalk designs) are painted on the floor as a sign of welcome. Fireworks are a key part of the celebrations, and people start to set them off days before the actual *Diwali* celebration takes place.

The most colourful of all Indian festivals is *Holi*. Celebrated by Hindus on the day after the full moon in early March, it marks the climax of spring. Processions with music, singing and dancing take place around temples. People light bonfires on the night before *Holi* to symbolize the end of winter and the destruction of the devil Holika. But the most fun takes place on the day of *Holi* itself, when it is traditional to throw coloured pigment (*gulal*) and water at anybody. No one objects. People wear their oldest clothes since the colours can stain, and for days after *Holi*, people walk around with the tell-tale signs of having been hit.

National holidays

26 January Republic Day (celebrates the declaration of the **republic** in 1950)
15 August Independence Day
2 October *Ghandi Jayanti* (Mahatma Gandhi's Birthday)
25 December Christmas Day

Revellers cover each other in brightly coloured pigment to celebrate the spring festival of **Holi**.

Food and drink

In a country as large as India and with such a diverse climate, it is not surprising that food varies from region to region. In north India and in the largely Muslim areas, the daily diet consists of meat, vegetables and Indian breads such as *naan* and *chapati* (see opposite). In strict Hindu families in the state of Gujarat, most people are vegetarian. In the south, fish is a staple in coastal areas, and rice is a more important part of the diet than in the north. South India is also home to the *thali*, a complete meal of vegetables, rice, Indian bread and even dessert served on the same plate.

A woman sells fresh puris (crispy, puffed-up, deep-fried bread) at her stand on the streets of Hampi in central southern India.

Usually every meal is freshly prepared, which means cooks spend a lot of time in the kitchen. There are staples that appear at every meal such as rice, Indian breads and *dhal*. *Dhal* is a thick stew usually made with dried lentils. It is very nutritious, and it is said there are as many variations of *dhal* as there are families in India.

India has its own 'fast food'. Street vendors sell popular snacks such as *bhelpuri*. *Bhelpuri* is made of thin, crispy lentil-flour noodles, puffed rice and wheat crackers mixed with diced boiled potatoes, chopped raw onion, coriander and different chutneys. It is the most popular snack in Mumbai, and street vendors have their own secret blends of ingredients. *Bhelpuri* is best eaten immediately, while everything is crispy.

India makes its own versions of soft drinks with names such as Thums Up! Indian drinks include freshly squeezed tropical fruit juices that can be bought from roadside sellers. A very refreshing drink is fresh coconut water, which is available everywhere in the south. Roadside sellers cut fresh green coconuts open with a machete. The coconut milk is then drunk through a straw. When the customer has finished drinking, the seller scrapes out the soft coconut flesh for the customer to eat. Lassi is a drink made of yoghurt thinned with water and with either salt or sugar added according to taste. Served with ice and a sprinkle of fresh cardamom spice, it is very refreshing on hot days. Hot tea, flavoured with spices and boiled with milk and sugar, is an extremely popular drink at any time of the year.

Many Indian desserts are milk-based. Some of the most popular are *kulfi*, an Indian version of ice-cream flavoured with cardamom, pistachio nuts and saffron; *gulab jamun*, which are spongy ground almond balls, deep fried and then soaked in a saffron syrup and eaten cold; and *firnee*, a rice and milk dessert served with almonds, raisins and pistachios. For those who prefer something lighter, there is fresh fruit such as mangoes, bananas, melons, tangerines, guavas, pomegranates and pineapples.

Chapatis

Chapatis are to India what chips are to the UK. They are very easy to prepare:

Mix wheat flour with water until the mixture can be rolled into a ball. Break off a little of the mixture and roll it into a thin circle. Heat a heavy-based frying pan but do not add any fat. When the pan is hot, put the *chapati* in and cook until it starts to puff up. Turn it over and cook the other side in the same way. Remove the chapati from the pan and serve while still warm. *Chapatis* can be served with any meal or as a snack with Indian chutneys or a salsa of diced tomato, onion, coriander and a squeeze of lemon.

There is great cross-fertilization between Christianity and Hinduism. In the state of Tamil Nadu, Christians do not eat beef or pork. In many places, Indian Christian women wear *tilak* dots on their foreheads.

The sixth-largest mosque in India, the Mecca Mosque in Hyderabad was built in 1598. Its central arch contains red bricks from Mecca.

RELIGIOUS LIFE

India is a secular nation, meaning that it has no official religion. Nevertheless, it is a deeply religious and spiritual country. Following independence and the **partition** of India, the country is now predominantly Hindu. Eighty per cent of Indians are Hindu, 14 per cent Muslim, 2.4 per cent Christian, 2 per cent Sikh and Buddhism now accounts for only 0.7 per cent. The rest of the population are Jains or belong to other religions. **Hinduism** and Buddhism, along with Jainism, which has approximately 5 million followers, are some of the world's oldest religions. Buddhism and Jainism were both started as a reaction to the rigid rules of Hinduism.

Islam

Although Muslims comprise only a small percentage of the population, there are more than 100 million Muslims in India, making it one of the largest Islamic populations in the world. **Islam** is a relatively young religion. It dates from the 7th century AD, when the religion's founder, the prophet Mohammed (AD 570–632), received revelations, or visions, from Allah (God). Mohammed's visions were written down and collected in what became Islam's holy book, the Koran. Muslims believe that the one God, Allah, who created the world, is all powerful and wise, and will one day bring the world into final judgement.

The Muslim holy day is Friday, and the main **mosque** (temple) in every city is known as the Friday mosque. Every male Muslim has to pray five times a day by facing towards Mecca in Saudi Arabia, Islam's holiest city. Once a year, every Muslim has to fast from sunrise to sunset for the month of Ramadan, and every Muslim must try to make a pilgrimage to Mecca.

Hinduism

Hinduism is the largest religion in Asia with more than 700 million followers in India alone. Hinduism is unusual compared to other world religions in that it has no founder or prophet and no central text or creed. Instead, Hinduism has evolved over many centuries, absorbing influences from other religions. As a result, its beliefs can seem complex and contradictory to outsiders. A person can only be born into Hinduism and, unlike most other world religions, one cannot convert to Hinduism. At birth, every Hindu belongs to a **caste** that he or she cannot leave (see page 114). The castes determine the social standing within the Hindu community. At the top of the caste system are the **Brahmins**, or priests. Next is the warrior caste, the *Kshatriyas*, who are either soldiers or administrators. Then the *Vaishyas*, who make up the artisan or

Hindu gods

Hinduism has many gods, of which the trinity of Brahma, Vishnu and Siva are the most important. Brahma is the creator; Vishnu is the preserver and sustainer. His incarnations are Rama and Krishna, the preserver. Siva is both creator and destroyer. Other gods are worshipped for different reasons. In Bengal, Kali, the goddess of destruction, has always been worshipped, and in Mumbai, Lakshmi, the goddess of wealth, is a favourite.

Two very popular gods that are seen all over India in temples and homes are the animal gods Ganesh, the elephant god, and Hanuman, the monkey god.

The caste system

The four castes are said to come from different parts of the creator Brahma's body: the Brahmins from his mouth, the *Kshatriyas* from his arms, the *Vaishyas* from his thighs and the *Shudras* from his feet. Beneath all these castes are the Untouchables, or *Dalits*. Their job is to perform tasks considered demeaning, including the cremation of the dead. Being born into one caste does not necessarily determine a person's occupation. For example, many Brahmin caste members are poor farmers. An Indian street cleaner, however, will almost always be a member of the *Dalits*. Discrimination against the *Dalits* was made illegal in 1947, but it still persists today. In an attempt to improve conditions for the *Dalits*, the government reserves a large number of public sector jobs and university places for this caste alone.

commercial class, followed by the *Shudras*, who are the farmers and peasant class.

Hindus believe that life is eternal and consists of a series of births that can be ended only by reaching spiritual salvation (*moksha*). Each reincarnation either leads closer or further away from salvation depending on **karma,** the law of good and bad causes. Good actions in life mean a step closer to stopping the rebirth cycle; bad actions mean further reincarnations. There are three basic religious practices in Hinduism: daily prayer (*puja*), cremation of the dead and the laws and practices of the caste system.

Founded in Persia (modern Iran) in the 6th century BC, Zoroastrianism involves worship of the god Ahur Mazda, who is symbolized by fire. In India followers are known as Parsees (because they originally came from Persia) and mostly live in Mumbai.

The beliefs of Hinduism were collected together in a set of texts called the *Vedas* (see page 46) between 1000 BC and AD 500, although they had been transmitted orally for many centuries prior to this. Later Hindu texts include the *Brahmanas*, which deal with sacrifice, and the *Aranyakas* or 'forest treatises'.

Buddhism

For several centuries Buddhism dominated the religious life of India. Although it originated in India and is still a major religion in other parts of Asia – notably parts of China and Japan – today Buddhism is largely confined to north-east India, although many important Buddhist monuments still exist throughout the country. Buddhism was founded in (about) 560 BC by Siddharta Gautama, known as the Buddha, a princely Hindu who had been born in present-day Nepal. Disenchanted with Hinduism, the Buddha formulated the concept of *dharma*, the true nature of the world and the teaching that there is no self. The only way to achieve the peaceful state of **nirvana** is to accept that everything in the material world is impermanent and subject to change. Nirvana is achieved by an eightfold path characterized by the renunciation of the material world and the search for a true understanding of human experience.

Sikhism

The Sikh religion is dominant in the Punjab, in north-west India. It shares elements with Hinduism and Islam but has a distinct identity from both. Sikhism's founder was Guru Nanak (1469–1539), who regarded the many gods of Hinduism as names of one supreme God. He preached that all people have the possibility of escaping the cycle of death and rebirth regardless of caste by becoming centred on God. Guru Nanak's teachings were further expounded by nine succeeding gurus during the centuries after his death.

Jainism

Jainism is based upon the teachings of Mahariva, who was active in the 6th century BC. Like Buddhism, it seeks escape from the endless cycle of rebirth, and this is achieved by following a path of austere living, meditation, care for all living things and rejection of impure action. The Jain population of about 5 million is today largely concentrated in the state of Gujarat in the north-west of India.

The Sikh brotherhood of khalsa *is represented by five emblems:* **kesh** *(unshorn hair),* **kangha** *(a comb),* **kaach** *(short trousers),* **kirpan** *(a sword) and* **kara** *(a steel bracelet, representing the link with God).*

The future

'India has the sanction of her own past glory and future vision to become strong – in every sense of the word.'

Indian Prime Minister Atal Behari Vajpayee

On the face of it, it might seem that India, as it starts the 21st century, is beset with problems. Its ever-growing population, the 1999 war with Pakistan over Kashmir, the rise of Hindu **fundamentalism** and regional demands for independence all suggest that India has a troubled future. However, thousands of years of experience have taught Indians many valuable lessons that should help them deal with, if not solve, their difficulties.

The most obvious problem facing India is its increasing population. By 2030, it will have overtaken China as the world's most populous nation. As the population grows, increasing pressure is put on India's infrastructure, such as its railways, roads and schools. Jobs, housing and food all become more difficult to find for everybody. India's forests are disappearing as people destroy natural habitats for food, fuel and housing.

India's relationship with Pakistan is another immediate concern. In 1999, the war between the two countries at Kargil, in Kashmir, and both countries' nuclear weapons testing saw relations worsen. During the 1990s, the Bharatiya Janata Party capitalized on anti-**Muslim** feeling and encouraged the rise of Hindu fundamentalism. This has led to some persecution of other religious minorities. Elsewhere across India – such as in the Punjab and in the south – people have agitated for independence, and the threat of localized conflict is never far away.

Many in India hope that small-scale industry will fire other areas of the economy and allow the country to capitalize on its vast workforce.

FACT FILE

- India's software industry became the country's biggest foreign currency earner in 2003.

- Less that 11% of India is still forested.

- India tested nuclear weapons in 1998 and 1999.

- Mumbai, Delhi, Kolkata and Chennai are all among the world's top 30 most populated cities.

- The cost of living in India is one of the lowest in the world – the third lowest behind Libya and Zimbabwe.

- India currently has 16% of the world's population living on 2.4% of the world's landmass.

Socially, India changed rapidly in the last fifteen years of the 20th century, largely because of the increased influence of **the West**. Foreign television programmes and the ability of more people to travel overseas were two major influences on Indian life. Today, particularly in middle-class families, there is a struggle between traditional Indian values and Western materialism and consumerism.

REASONS FOR OPTIMISM?

Despite the problems, there are reasons to think that India's future will be bright. Although the population continues to rise, Indian women are having fewer children. The chief reason for the continuing population rise is that Indians are living longer as hygiene and medical care improve. Despite having so many mouths to feed, India is self-sufficient in food production. In 1998, food grain production hit a record 181 million tonnes (178 million tons).

In the 1999 elections, the BJP downplayed its anti-Muslim and pro-Hindu attitude, emphasizing instead its pledge to open up more of the economy to private investors. The party recognized that it would gain more political success from promoting the economy than

Ecological issues

India's developing economy presents new problems for the country's ecology. Deforestation is a major problem, and less than 11% of India's dense forests remain. Local nature reserves may often fail to get the protection they require because of the corruption of local politicians. Delhi and Mumbai are among the most polluted cities on Earth, and levels of carbon monoxide in Delhi can reach as high as fifty times the recommended levels of the World Health Organization. The problem is compounded by the use of old and inefficient machines and vehicles.

In comparison to Western Europe or the USA, however, national levels of pollution are low. While the rate of increase is alarming, it will take India at least twenty years before the country's emissions of carbon dioxide begin to approach those of the USA.

from stirring up religious differences. India's economy is, of course, crucial to the country's future. The seeds for growth have been sown – in 1999, the stock market hit record highs, inflation was very low and the economy grew. With such a huge domestic market, India is seen by many in the West as a potential economic superpower.

Despite the fact that almost half the country cannot read or write, India has one of the world's best university systems. It produces a huge number of postgraduate students, and most university courses are taught in English. High levels of knowledge and the use of the English language have helped bring about India's information technology (**IT**) revolution. In 1998, total software **exports** totalled £1625 million, despite the fact that the market is still in its infancy. Indians possess the knowledge and technical capability to progress far into the IT market. It is hoped that a trickle-down effect will occur – that is, that the growth of the industry will create jobs for Indians all over the country, not just in the IT centres. Despite the importance of the IT industry, India only had 100,000 Internet connections in 1998, a tiny figure considering the population of the country. A major problem in India is the unreliability of the national telephone system. As a result of this problem, the government set aside £187.5 million to invest in updating the country's telecommunications system.

The key to India's future lies in its people and their capacity for hard work and study. India's vast workforce makes it an obvious player in the world economy, and the cost of paying this workforce remains so low that India is able to undercut many of its economic rivals. The growth of domestic industry means that while skilled Indians used to move overseas to further their career, they are now able to stay in India to achieve the same goal. Their presence should help the less well-off and less educated in India. Taxes that they pay will go to the Indian government rather than to foreign governments, and their greater spending power should boost the Indian economy further.

In 1998, the USA imposed sanctions against India for its testing of nuclear weapons and for escalating the arms race with Pakistan. The sanctions appeared to put a brake on international investment at that time.

Almanac

POLITICAL

country name:
    official long form: Republic
    of India
    short form: India
    local form: *Bharat*

nationality:
    noun: Indian(s)
    adjective: Indian

official language: Hindi and sixteen
    other official languages,
    including English

capital city: Delhi

type of government: federal republic

suffrage (voting rights): everyone
    eighteen years and over

national anthem: '*Jana Gana Mana*'
    ('Thou art the ruler')

national holiday: 26 January
    (Anniversary of Proclamation of
    the Republic)

flag:

GEOGRAPHICAL

location: southern Asia; latitudes
    8° to 37° north and longitudes
    68° to 98° east

climate: temperate in north, tropical
    monsoon in south

total area: 3,287,590 sq km
    (2,042,870 sq miles)
    land: 90%
    water: 10%

coastline: 7000 km (4350 miles)

terrain: mountains in north, desert in
    west, flat plains in east, upland
    plain in south (Deccan Plateau)

highest point: Mount Kangchenjunga,
    8586 m (28,169 ft)
lowest point: coastline on the Indian
    Ocean, 0 m

natural resources: coal, iron ore,
    manganese, mica bauxite,
    titanium ore, chromite,
    natural gas, diamonds,
    petroleum, limestone

land use (2000 est.):
    arable land: 56%

forests and woodland: 23%

permanent pastures: 4%

permanent crops: 1%

other: 16%

POPULATION

population (2003 est.): 1045 million

population density: 308 people per
sq km (496 per sq mile)

population growth rate (2002 est.):
1.51%

birth rate (2002 est.): 23.79 births
per 1000 of the population

death rate (2002 est.): 8.62 deaths
per 1000 of the population

sex ratio (2002 est.): 107 males per
100 females

total fertility rate (2002 est.): 2.98
children born for every woman
in the population

infant mortality rate (2002 est.):
61.5 deaths per 1000 live births

life expectancy at birth (2002 est.):
total population: 63.23 years
male: 62.55 years
female: 63.93 years

literacy:
total population: 52%
male: 65.5%
female: 37.7%

ECONOMY

currency: Indian rupee (Re);
1 Re = 100 paise

exchange rate (2002):
£1 = 68.34 rupees

gross national product (1999):
£223,125 million (fifteenth-
largest economy in the world)

average annual growth rate:
(1990–99): 6%

GNP per capita (1999 est.): £231

average annual inflation rate:
(1990–2000): 9%

unemployment rate: widespread
unemployment

exports (1999): £2125 million
imports (1999): £2562.5 million

foreign aid received (1998): £1813 million

Human Development Index
(an index scaled from 0 to 100 combining statistics
indicating adult literacy, years of schooling, life
expectancy and income levels):
56.3 (UK 91.8)

TIMELINE – INDIA

World history

Indian history

c.50,000 BC

c.40,000 Modern
humans – *Homo
sapiens sapiens* –
emerge

c.2000–1200 BC
Period of Minoan,
Hittite and
Mycaenean
Mediterranean
expansion

c.2500 BC
Harappa civilization
flourishes on banks
of Indus River

c.2300–2000 BC
Harappa civilization
trades with ancient
Sumeria

c.1500 BC
Aryans begin
to move south
through India

c.753 BC Rome
founded

c.1500–1200 BC
Vedic scriptures
written

c.500 BC

499–494 BC
Revolt of Ionian
cities against
Persian rule
leads to rise of
Classical Greece

c.500 BC
Emergence of
Buddhism in India

326 BC Alexander
the Great reaches
India but does
not conquer
the region

c.1350–1550
Italian
Renaissance leads
to rebirth of the
arts and classical
learning in Europe

c.1000 Vikings
reach American
continent but
do not settle

c.632–1530
Period of Islamic
expansion in
Middle East,
Europe and
North Africa

476 Fall of Rome
to the Goths

c.AD 1
Birth of Christ

c.112 BC Chinese
open Silk Route in
the East

146 BC Fall of
Carthage begins
Mediterranean
expansion of
Roman empire

1398 Tamerlane
the Great makes
raids on India

1206 Delhi
Sultanate
established

c.1000 Mahmud
of Ghazna begins
raids on India

c.1000

8th century
Muslim traders
establish bases
on west coast

7th century
Rajputs a major
power in north-
west India

AD 320 Gupta
empire founded

AD 0

190 BC Bactrian
Greeks begin 400
years of foreign
invasions in India

232 BC Death of
Emperor Asoka

321–184 BC
Period of Mauryan
empire

350 BC

c.1500

1492 Columbus lands in America

1520 Birth of Protestantism – the Pope expels Martin Luther from the Catholic Church

1642–51 English Civil War

1498 Vasco da Gama lands at Calicut

1527 Babur founds Mughal empire

1605 Death of Akbar

***c.*1700** Decline of Mughals and rise of Maratha empire

2000 The West celebrates the Millennium – 2000 years since the birth of Christ

1989 Communism collapses in eastern Europe

1999 Indian nuclear tests

1998 BJP comes to power

1991 Rajiv Gandhi is assassinated

1984 Indira Gandhi is assassinated

1975 State of Emergency

1971 Secession of Bangladesh

1966 Indira Gandhi becomes prime minister

1962 China invades India

1948 Gandhi is assassinated

1947 Independence and Partition of India

c.1750

***c.*1750** Industrial Revolution begins in England

1789 French Revolution begins

1815 Battle of Waterloo

1756–63 Seven Years' War between Britain and France for control of India

1857 Indian mutiny against British rule

1858 British government announces policy of support for princely states

1885 First Indian National Congress meets in Delhi

1905 Partition of Bengal

1919 Amritsar massacre

1969 First man lands on the moon

1963–75 Vietnam War

1957 Foundation of the European Economic Community (EEC)

1947

1914 World War One begins

1917 Revolution in Russia leads to establishment of Soviet Union

1918 World War One ends

1945 End of World War Two, defeat of Germany

1939 World War Two begins

1929 Wall Street Crash, beginning of Great Depression

1946 Muslim League's Direct Action Day

1937 Congress Party wins spectacular victory in elections

1930 Gandhi's Salt March

1920

Glossary

ashram Hindu centre for religious learning and spiritual practice

ayurvedic referring to a system of medicine based on the Vedic scriptures

Brahmin member of the highest, priestly caste

capitalism economic system based on supply and demand, and private ownership of businesses and industry

caste person's social level, determined by their birth

coalition alliance of one or more political parties, usually to form a government

communism social and political system based on a planned economy in which goods and land are owned by everyone and in which there is no private property

constitution written collection of a country's laws, its citizens' rights and beliefs

dharma (**Hindi**) sense of religious and social duties in Hinduism and the path of truth in Buddhism

export product that is sold to another country

fundamentalism strict adherence to the basic beliefs of a religion, usually involving the exclusion of other belief systems

ghats (**Hindi**) flight of steps leading to river

Harappan referring to the earliest known civilization in India, *c.*2500 BC

Hindi most widely spoken of India's seventeen national languages

Hinduism historic religion of India, based on many gods and originating in the second millennium BC

import product that is bought from another country

industrial describing an economy based on developed industries and infrastructure rather than on agriculture

Islam religion founded in Arabia in the 7th century based on obedience to Allah

IT information technology

karma balance between good and bad actions, determining a person's status or caste at rebirth

Lok Sabha lower house of the Indian Parliament

maharaja Indian king

maidan open green space

manufacturing process of turning simple, basic materials into complex goods

masala literally means 'mix', a type of Indian film that includes various different types of narrative

masjid mosque

monsoon period of intense rainfall occurring in India between June and October

mosque Muslim place of worship

multinational company or corporation having divisions in more than one country

mural wall painting

Muslim follower of the teachings of Islam

nationalization taking of private companies or corporations into public ownership

nirvana state of peaceful happiness and freedom from rebirth in Buddhism

open market market without tariffs (a charge imposed by government to limit certain types of trade) or other trade barriers

partition separation of pre-1947 India into the three separate areas of India and East and West Pakistan

Raj literally means 'rule', the period of British rule in India, lasting from the 18th century until 1947

Rajya Sabha upper house of the Indian Parliament

republic government in which the citizens of a country hold supreme power and where all the citizens of the country are equal under the law

sadhu Hindu holy man

sanctions withdrawal of trade or other economic provision in protest at a particular political action; usually enacted by one country upon another

Sanskrit ancient language of India

Sikhism religion founded in the 16th century based on the teachings of Guru Nanak

sitar long-necked string instrument that is played by plucking

shanty ramshackle dwelling made from found materials, usually on the edges of a large town

socialism economic and political system founded on public or state ownership of the means of production

tabla set of two small drums played with the hands

the West countries of western Europe and North America

Vedic referring to the *Vedas*, a series of ancient religious texts that were composed between 1500 and 1200 BC

Bibliography

Major sources used for this book
Craven, Ros, *Indian Art* (Thames and Hudson, 1998)
French, Patrick, *Liberty or Death* (Flamingo, 1994)
Spear, Percival, *History of India Volume II* (Penguin, 1992)
Thapar, Romila, *History of India Volume I* (Penguin, 1994)

General further reading
Bennett, Lynda A. (ed.), *Encyclopedia of World Cultures* (G. K. Hall & Co., 1992)
The Kingfisher History Encyclopedia (Kingfisher, 1999)
Student Atlas (Dorling Kindersley, 1998)
The World Book Encyclopedia (Scott Fetzer Company, 1999)

Further reading about India
Brown, Dale M (ed.), *Ancient India: Land of Mystery* (Time Life, 1995)

Cawthorne, Nigel, *The Art of India* (Laurel Glen, 1997)
Rai, Raghu (ed.), *A Day in the Life of India* (Collins Pub.; 1996)

Some websites about India
High Commission of India, London
    www.hcilondon.org
www.welcometoindia.com/home.html
www.britannica.com (type in 'India' in the search field)
www.mrdowling.com/612india.html
www.pbs.org/edens/anamalai
www.angelfire.com/in/myindia/tajmahal.html
http://rubens.anu.edu.au/student.projects/tajmahal/home.html

Index

Acknowledgements

Cover photo credit
Corbis

Photo credits
AKG London: Nou, Jean-Louis 44, 48, 54, 72 **Colin Tilley Loughrey:** 18, 20, 76, 88, 110 **Corbis:** Dave Bartruff 89, Betteman 67, 68, 71, Burnstein Collection 92, Stephanie Colasanti 30, Peter Guttman 99, Lindsay Hebberd 93, 109, Robert Holmes 40, Jeremy Homer 51, Hulton-Deutsch Collection 65, Catherine Karnow 32, 81, 101, 106, Earl & Nazima Kowall 38, 115, Charles & Josetta Lenars 19, 21 Chris Lisle 12, Philadelphia Museum 94, Richard Powers 103, Chris Rainer 84, Dave Samuel Robbins 15, Galen Rowell 90, Francesco Venturi/Kea Publishing Services 37, Staffan Widstrand 28, Adam Woolfitt 96 **Hulton Getty:** 69 **Hutchison:** Carluz Freire 112, Goycoolea 66, John Hatt 29, Julie Mighet 1, 34, C. Pemberton 33 **Peter Newark's Military Pictures:** 53 **Robert Hunt Library:** 61 **Still Pictures:** 116 **Tony Stone:** Glen Allison 6, Anthony Cassidy 78, Chris Haigh 98, Adrian Murrell 80, Manoj Shah 26 **Tony Tilley:** 82 **Werner Forman Archive:** Victoria & Albert Museum 58, De Young Museum, San Francisco 113